PRAISE FOR SARAH SELECKY AND
STORY IS A STATE OF MIND

"The accumulated inspiration and practical wisdom in this book, so essential to writers, is as wide-ranging and comprehensive as it is accessible; in fact, what Sarah Selecky offers here is nothing short of remarkable. As a true companion and ally, her two decades of intimate writing, listening, and teaching can be found on every page. Given that there is nothing else quite like it, the only thing left to say is read it and write!"

—Peter Levitt, author of *Fingerpainting on the Moon*

"This generous exploration of the creative process inspires you to create the beautiful empty space in which you can breathe and write. Sarah Selecky's practices are deceptively simple—and they apply to many art forms beyond writing. She teaches that the most important instrument an artist possesses is curiosity. To wonder, explore, and discover that which you didn't even know you knew!"

—Stephen Nachmanovitch, author of *The Art of Is* and *Free Play*

"*Story Is a State of Mind* by Sarah Selecky is a brilliant, soulful, transformative guide to the craft of writing. Filled with powerful exercises and practical wisdom, Sarah helps writers explore their creativity, set boundaries (my biggest challenge), and cultivate the discipline needed to finish their work (my second biggest challenge). Having had the privilege of teaching alongside Sarah, I can personally attest to her talent and deep understanding of the writing process. I'm currently working on my eleventh book and struggling to find my groove, so this book comes at just the right time for me! *Story Is a State of Mind* is an essential companion for anyone serious about their writing journey."

—Theresa Reed, author of *The Cards You're Dealt*

"Savvy and persuasive, prize-winning fiction writer Sarah Selecky takes readers on a magic journey through the world of writerly craft. Both beginning writers and veterans will find useful tips and insights in her charming book about the art of transforming the blank page into a story."

—Susan Swan, author of *The Dead Celebrities Club*

"*Story Is a State of Mind* illuminates the sacred intersection between craft and consciousness. Sarah Selecky guides writers to approach their work with both rigor and reverence, offering practices that engage body, mind, and spirit. This guide shows us how to blend technical skill with intuitive wisdom, turning the act of writing into a transformative practice. An essential companion for anyone seeking to write with magic."

—Maia Toll, author of *Letting Magic In* and *The Night School*

"Through generous counsel, illuminating exercises, and a big helping of magic, *Story Is a State of Mind* by Sarah Selecky shows us how creativity can be cultivated and sustained for a fertile—and joyful—writing process. It also happens to be terrifically well-written. In warm, humorous prose, Selecky gently reconnects us with creative curiosity, asking a fundamental question: What if you approached your writing as play? Read this book, and I promise you will find the answer."

—Emily Urquhart, author of *Ordinary Wonder Tales* and
The Age of Creativity

"A thoughtful, meditative guide to storytelling that will help bring focus to creatives who are feeling lost in our noisy world. *Story Is a State of Mind* will bring ease to your writing practice and help you answer the creative call."

—Carly Watters, literary agent and co-host of
The Sh*t No One Tells You About Writing podcast

STORY IS A STATE OF MIND

STORY IS A STATE OF MIND

WRITING AND THE ART OF CREATIVE CURIOSITY

SARAH SELECKY

Assembly Press

PRINCE EDWARD COUNTY, ONTARIO

Library and Archives Canada Cataloguing in Publication

Title: Story is a state of mind : writing and the art of creative curiosity / Sarah Selecky.
Names: Selecky, Sarah Lucille, 1974- author
Identifiers: Canadiana (print) 20240485564 | Canadiana (ebook) 20240486382 | ISBN 9781998336012 (softcover) | ISBN 9781998336029 (EPUB)
Subjects: LCSH: Authorship. | LCSH: Creation (Literary, artistic, etc.) | LCGFT: Essays.
Classification: LCC PN145 .S45 2025 | DDC 808.02—dc23

Published by Assembly Press | assemblypress.ca
Cover and interior designed by Greg Tabor
Edited by Andrew Faulkner

Printed and bound in Canada on uncoated paper made from 100% recycled content in line with our commitment to ethical business practices and sustainability.

For you

CONTENTS

✎ includes practice exercise

*

INVITATION

Pause for a moment.

Wherever you are right now, make yourself a bit more comfortable.

Take in a deep inhale. Notice how this air feels as it comes into your chest.

Exhale. Notice how this air feels as you release it.

This moment, right now, is an invitation.

An invitation to slow down.

An invitation to pay attention to how you think about writing.

To sense the subtle shifts in your body as your thoughts form and take shape in your mind.

Like clouds, these thoughts are constantly moving and changing.

Breathe in and out normally.

Watch the clouds gather and shift.

Now ask yourself a question:

Can I think and feel at the same time?

As a writer, you know how to use language well. You excel at communication, analysis, and problem-solving. Your mind loves working with words and ideas, but your body, with its instincts and sensations, holds wisdom, too. As a creative writer, you have the rare ability to bridge these realms and work with both thoughts and feelings at once. While this can be challenging, it's a skill that you can develop. When you cultivate this skill, you open doors to new dimensions in your creative work.

This book is a guide to lighting up your creative neurology. You will learn how to bridge the gap between your intellectual strengths and your physical intuition and go into a space where thought and feeling are combined. This is where the magic of writing comes alive.

Listen closely.

Right now, your body is telling you something your mind has yet to name with words.

What is it?

How can you know it if there is no word for it?

Pay attention. Notice without language.

Take another inhale, then exhale.

It's normal not to have a word for this feeling.

It's okay not to know exactly what it is.

Notice the sensation of your breath as it moves through your body.

Try to feel the air in your chest.

Does it feel warm or cool? Heavy or light?

This is where your story begins.

Story isn't just something we write—it's a state of mind. This book is an invitation to inhabit that state of mind.

In these pages, you'll rediscover the power of words as living, breathing elements that resonate through your entire being. You'll learn how to tune into physical sensations as you think, to help bring unexpressed feelings and sensations into words. You'll practise cognitive reframing and learn how to recognize your negative thoughts to quiet them, or to turn them into creative and curious ones.

You'll start to cultivate curiosity as a tangible, felt experience, and use it—along with the powers of your intellect and intuition—to take your writing to thrilling new places. The practices you'll find in this book will allow you to connect to your creative unconscious mind to access a wealth of resources you didn't know you had.

You'll work on setting and keeping boundaries in your schedule. We'll talk about influences and how to read effectively as a writer. We'll look at how to reliably finish the projects you start, how to revise and edit using power instead of force, and how to make sure you're giving yourself the rest you need so you feel energized and ready when it's time to share your work with others.

Your state of mind will shift during and through your writing practice. As you bring your whole self—mind, body, and intuition—into your work, you'll likely discover that your craft improves organically, without the need to compartmentalize or force your progress. You'll learn how to get out of your own way in order to feel calm, fascinated, and curious in your writing life. You might find that writing feels more natural, and what you write may even surprise you. This holistic method of writing can feel like a revelation—a way of creating that honours both your artistic growth and your innate wisdom.

Let this book be your compass, your mirror, your coach, your companion.

This is an invitation to write with your entire being.

*

CREATIVE CURIOSITY

I've always known I wanted to write. As a kid, I read everything from C. S. Lewis to V. C. Andrews. I started writing down my thoughts pretty much as soon as I learned how to hold a pencil. When I was a teenager, I crammed journals and diaries with my loopy handwriting. I loved writing and writing loved me. We were best friends.

In my late teens, I began to write my first real short stories, and I tried to get them published. I sent my work to *Sassy* and *Seventeen*, and to local newspapers and contests. Looking back, I can see now that this changed everything—and not in the way you might think. Sending work out to editors is an important part of being a writer, and I'm glad I did it. But there was a consequence to these efforts that I couldn't predict.

As soon as I began writing stories to get them published, I started to disconnect from my curiosity. The change in my relationship with writing was so subtle, I didn't even notice it at first. But the separation gradually grew, until it became a painful tension. I began to resist doing the thing I loved most.

As an emerging writer, my weeks went like this: When I was able to write, everything felt okay. But when I wasn't writing, I felt like there was something wrong with me. I became anxious and depressed, and my thoughts twisted into glum, gluey knots. I heard this was called writer's block, but that didn't seem to reflect the deep heartbreak that I was experiencing. This felt like being in a fight with someone I loved.

It took me twenty years to learn what this pattern was and how to change it.

During those years in the wilderness, I had gone slightly off track. I was highly focused on getting my writing published, and so I put all of my mental and emotional attention on that goal. I believed that this would give my creative work value, and I focused directly on this kind of achievement and accomplishment. Getting published is an excellent goal for a writer! The problem was that I'd stopped nourishing my own creative curiosity. The intensity of my goal of becoming a published author pushed me out of balance. I spent those years writing for someone else: an editor I hadn't met yet, a projection of literary authority I created in my mind. I was writing pieces that I hoped sounded like publishable stories, trying to guess what readers would want, and what editors thought was important. In the process, I'd forgotten what made me want to be a writer in the first place.

I used to write because I loved reading. I used to write because I was curious about the way words and sentences could work alchemically on a page to create character, emotion, and mystery. I used to love the way it felt when I put my pen to paper. My body would relax as I wrote by hand in my notebook, and then my mind would awaken. Writing poems and stories used to reliably bring me to a state of calm fascination. I used to write to connect to myself, and to connect to something bigger than myself.

I missed that connection. I felt far away from that calm, awakened state of mind I had as a young writer. Now it was as though I was searching for connection in the form of an acceptance letter. This was a lonely feeling. I began to wonder: *How do I reconnect to what I love about writing?*

That question led me on a journey of rediscovery, not just as a writer but also as an explorer searching for new ways of thinking. I lived in remote forested areas that had limited access to cities and culture. I went on annual ten-day silent meditation retreats. I got my MFA in creative writing. I studied neurolinguistic programming. I studied with masters in different fields to learn new ways of thinking about consciousness, language, story, and wonder. In search of creative flow and happiness, I learned from novelists, poets, creativity and life coaches, psychotherapists, running instructors, story doctors, play theory specialists, yoga teachers, sleep coaches, psychics, astrologers, energy healers, scientists, hypnotherapists, and sociologists.

I learned two important things in my exploration. First: In my consciousness, happiness and curiosity show up together. They are deeply entwined. Second: Being curious was not just a personality trait. It was an active practice.

As I worked through my own creative blocks, I realized that my struggle wasn't unique. Many writers lose touch with their initial passion and creativity in the pursuit of external validation. This realization drew me to teaching. I began to share the practices I'd learned with other writers who, like me, wanted to experiment with their creativity and consciousness. What began as small writing classes in my living room soon grew into something much larger. Year after year, these intimate gatherings filled up with writers seeking guidance, connection, and a way back to their love of writing.

Through teaching, I gained more insights into the mental knots that seemed to make so many writers unhappy. I learned how to untangle these complex issues, not just for myself, but for others, too. The truth is that writing itself isn't so difficult when we're fully present and engaged, when our mind and body are aligned and in flow. But the way we think about writing can take us right out of that alignment. In other words, writing isn't hard. It's *thinking* about writing that makes it hard.

As demand for my classes grew, I expanded my reach and founded the Sarah Selecky Writing School to meet the needs of writers seeking help, beyond the borders of my living room. At the same time, I was putting these practices to work in my own life. My first book of short stories was nominated for a prestigious literary award, and my novel was optioned for a premium series on HBO. I developed a writing program that garnered critical acclaim, with graduates who went on to get published and win literary awards themselves. Looking back, I can see that my best creative work has always come from tending to my curiosity—listening to it, nurturing it, and allowing it to grow.

As an author, I've experienced the highs and lows of getting my writing published, rejected, celebrated, and panned. It's been a roller coaster of learning. But it's my role as a creative writing teacher, mindset coach, and mentor that has truly deepened my understanding of the unique challenges writers face in their creative process.

I don't think that being a writer is supposed to be easy, but I do believe that knowing how to stay connected to your creative energy makes it much more interesting and fulfilling. A writing life is full of adventure, paradox, tension, and uncomfortable oppositional energy. These are all elements we appreciate in the stories we love. The challenges are real. They are also opportunities for your personal growth, should you choose them.

Since I started teaching online, I've been writing bimonthly blog posts about how to face these challenges, addressing the gnarliest blocks and problems that plague the writers in my community. These letters, combined with a variety of programs I lead both online and in person through my writing school, have allowed me to connect with and support countless writers on their creative journeys. This book is the culmination of my years of experience with creativity, language, and meditation as both a writer and an educator. It's a distillation of the lessons I've learned, the techniques I've developed, and the insights I've gained from working with writers at all stages of their careers.

As I revisited some of my earlier newsletters in writing this book, I found myself revising and updating them to align with everything I've learned since I first wrote them. I keep learning new ways to understand writing! Curiosity does that: it's always evolving, pushing me into new territory, expanding my understanding. I know there is much more to discover, and at the same time, I'm excited to share these practices with you so you can use them in your writing life now.

Curiosity is thrilling because it actively reveals possibilities that exist beyond what we know or expect for ourselves. I experienced this firsthand after my novel was optioned for television. Despite this success, I found myself creatively paralyzed, tethered to a project I wasn't actively working on. Instead, I entered a time of endless waiting (there is a lot of waiting involved in the option process), and I felt a strange numbness whenever I tried to write something new.

I had made a commitment to lead a Story Is a State of Mind retreat that summer, and I showed up for it plagued by self-doubt. How could I teach creative writing to forty people when I was personally feeling so stuck? I guided my students through the practices I'd designed to awaken curiosity and I worked through the exercises myself, expecting a continuation of the blankness I'd been feeling for months. To my wonder and delight, the practices rekindled my own creative spark. I didn't get a new idea for a book right away, but I did enter a new state of mind—I was curious and open. From there, I began writing again and felt surprised and engaged by my new work.

Our creative practices work even when we don't believe they will. This is the power of showing up and engaging with them: They can guide us, surprise us, and create change, despite ourselves. We show up, we practise, and we open ourselves to new possibilities. That's the gift I hope this book offers you: a way into that state of mind where you feel open and pleasantly surprised, even when—especially when—you feel stuck.

This is an embodied and balanced approach to creative writing that integrates your analytical and imaginative thinking at the same time. When you write in this state, you're connected to and fuelled by what I call *creative curiosity*. Creative curiosity is a mindset of open exploration and wonder through which you actively seek out the true nature and direction of your writing project.

As you write with your creative curiosity, you can better connect to your own true nature, too. This means that what you write in this state of mind will be enriched by the depth and intelligence of your presence. This is the magic that brings your craft to life.

For most writers, working with creative curiosity doesn't always happen by default. It's something we do with intention, and tend to consistently, like keeping a garden. If you stop paying attention to your creative curiosity, it can be hard to access it when you need it. This is good news because it means that you can strengthen your connection simply by paying attention to it more often.

I love teaching people how to cultivate and take care of their creative curiosity, and I love seeing the changes in their lives when they do: they're happier, more focused, and lit up by the puzzles they encounter as they improve their craft and technique. And, of course, I celebrate when they get published, too.

Whether you're a successful author struggling to reconnect with what you used to love about writing or you're new to creative writing and uncertain about where to begin, the essays and practices in this book will meet you where you are.

They'll show you how to reliably move forward in your writing life right now, while ensuring you stay connected to the joy and fascination that drew you to writing in the first place.

If you ever feel cloudy, confused, or alienated from your writing, these essays are here to remind you that the light of your love for writing is still glowing brightly, even if you feel disconnected from it. The practices in this book will help you fly above the clouds, so you can always reconnect to that bright sunshine.

I'm glad you're here. If you're ready to fall in love with writing again, keep reading.

*

HOW TO USE THIS BOOK

The advice, coaching, and practices in this book are designed to benefit all writers, regardless of genre. The core principles of tapping into creative curiosity, cultivating whole-minded-ness, and writing from a flow state are universally applicable. I write fiction, so many of my examples and exercises are drawn from that experience—the work of conjuring characters and their worlds out of thin air. But these techniques can support and enhance any form of creative writing. If you write creative non-fiction, poetry, or memoir, you will also find gold in here.

The essays are organized with a logic meant to run parallel to the process of writing and revising a book-length project, from what you need to know at the start, what will help you stay motivated in the middle, to how to complete, edit, and share your work. But these lessons and practices are cyclical, non-linear, and overlapping. There is no step-by-step method to follow. These practices are meant to be repeated, and reading these essays is like taking your daily vitamins.

You can read these essays in linear order or close your eyes and flip the book open at random for a surprise burst of motivation. Follow your curiosity. (If the statement "Follow your curiosity" is frustrating, that's okay—it's a sign that you're on the edge of your comfort zone. Take a deep breath, remind yourself that growth happens when we stretch ourselves, and encourage yourself to explore. Even tiny steps outside your usual patterns can lead to big creative breakthroughs.)

This isn't a creative writing class or an instruction manual. Instead, I'm giving you a variety of practices that you can try on for size and make a part of your life, similar to lifting weights, meditating, or brushing your teeth.

When you encounter a practice, don't just read it and move on to the next thing—do it. This book uses experiential learning to help you physically feel how your writing is or isn't working, which can only happen by completing the exercises.

As you develop a deeper awareness of your own creative mindset, you'll collect tools and insights to help navigate your own path. When you encounter rough patches or moments of doubt, these practices can give you the means to realign yourself and to go back to the page with renewed purpose and clarity. Start your day with a practice that interests you, and then come back to it consistently to see what you learn from doing it over time.

However you choose to engage with it, my hope is that this book will help guide you toward a deeper sense of creative fulfillment.

*

WHAT YOU NEED

All you need to experience this book is a quiet space to read and write, two notebooks—a bullet journal for tracking and notes and a blank one for freewriting—a writing instrument, and a timer.

Your space can be a little desk you set up in your bedroom or kitchen, a café in a part of town you don't frequent that often, a library, or your living room sofa. As long as it's a place where you can be comfortable and uninterrupted, it's perfect.

I recommend using a bullet journal to easily keep track of the exercises in this book, to make notes, and to document your learning journey. Bullet journals often have dotted pages, which offer flexibility for various tracking methods. For your freewriting practice (where you generate your new ideas and explore setting, character, and scene), choose a separate notebook with your preferred page style—lined, blank, or dotted. This way, you'll have dedicated spaces for the different parts of your writing practice.

If you don't already have these notebooks, choose new ones to use exclusively alongside this book. It will be easier to refer to your completed exercises and their outcomes.

I like to write on blank paper the best, but lined or dotted paper gives me more structure when I feel the need for it. It really depends on my mood and what I happen to be writing about. I prefer thicker paper when I write with wet ink so it doesn't bleed through the page. My favourite notebook size is one that fits in my purse, so I can take it with me easily. Experiment with notebook size and paper weight to see what works best for you.

I want you to write by hand. I prefer writing longhand for a number of reasons (keep reading, I'll explain them later in this book). Please choose a pen that glides easily over the page without much effort. I personally find ballpoint pens sticky and slow, and writing with them makes my hand and wrist tire more easily. A pencil, lightweight fountain pen, gel pen, or rollerball are all perfect for writing by hand.

Use an old-fashioned egg timer or some other analog device to keep track of your time. The key is to find a timer that's not connected to your phone, so you won't be interrupted or distracted during your writing practice.

Keep an open mind. Try everything once, just to see what happens, then revisit the practices in this book that work best for you. Stay hydrated. Remember to breathe. And enjoy yourself!

*

WRITE WITHOUT THINKING

Creative writers face a unique paradox: We use language to express the inexpressible. We transform wordless experiences into words. "Happiness compresses time, makes it dense and bright, pocketsized," writes Ann Patchett.

We can paint visual pictures, play soundscapes, evoke emotions, and create sensory experiences of flavour and texture using language alone. "But I am not calm," writes Deborah Levy. "My mind is like the edge of motorways where foxes eat the owls at night."

Our creative challenge is most profound when we encounter moments that leave us speechless—these are often the very experiences we feel compelled to capture in words. "It was a fine cry—loud and long—but it had no bottom and it had no top, just circles and circles of sorrow," writes Toni Morrison.

Other art forms don't use language in the same way. Dancers can create their art by moving their bodies through space, no words required. A pianist can evoke powerful emotions through their instrument alone. Visual artists may intellectually structure a conceptual piece of art, but the moment they put their hands on the clay, the paint, or the digital photograph, they are able to work wordlessly to get their message across. They can often bypass language entirely, letting their physical actions and sensory experiences guide their creative process.

But language and thinking are deeply intertwined for writers. Writers must use the very tool of thought—language—to create their art, and this can make it difficult to separate the process from the product. This is the challenge that lies at the heart of our practice: How do we transform abstract ideas and sensory experiences into concrete language without thinking?

We need to cultivate our cognitive flexibility so we can move fluidly between different modes of thinking. There's an interplay between writing and thought, and a delight that comes from using language to get to something that lies beyond language. So, we practise. When it's time, we enjoy our performance. Afterwards, we do some deep stretches and soak our feet. Then we turn on the music and start our practice again.

*

WHITE SPACE

As a writer, your mental focus—your capacity for attention—is one of your greatest resources.

The human capacity for attention is limited. On any given day, there are more demands on your attention than you can effectively handle. So if you're going to write, you have to make a choice: What will you stop doing so you can save your attention for writing?

Choosing where you put your attention is always a powerful act. But before smartphones and addictive technology like the infinite scroll were invented, writers used to have access to more language-free time without having to actively make this decision.

I grew up in the 1980s and I wrote my first novel on a word processor when I was in high school. I was assigned my first email account in 1995 as a university undergrad. I got to live through the cultural transition from a pre-digital era to a digital one, which means that, like my fellow Gen-Xers, I am wired to understand both pre-digital and digital types of mental connectivity.

Living through this shift showed me that the way we think isn't set in stone. Our brains can learn different modes of consciousness. This made me curious about the phenomenon of awareness, especially as it pertained to my creative writing. I practised paying attention to my attention, and found that the more I practised, the more I could understand, adapt, and tend to my state of mind by choice.

I really noticed this shift when I began communicating, socializing, and teaching online. It used to be that times of transition—taking the streetcar, standing in line at the grocery store, and sitting in waiting rooms—were moments when ideas would come to me most often. Now I find myself checking my phone whenever I have a spare second.

As a creative writing teacher, I work with a lot of people who struggle with distraction and attention burnout. This phenomenon has grown steadily since I started teaching in 2001. One writer I worked with admitted with sadness that she feared she was getting "dumber" as she got older, that her sentences weren't as textured as they used to be. Another confessed that she was finding it difficult to focus when reading the longer essays she used to love. We're writers! If we can't focus enough to write and read, who can?

The answer is that we all need more white space in our lives—moments of clarity and calm that allow our creative curiosity to emerge.

We need time spent staring into middle distance. We need to admire tendrils of steam as they rise from a teacup, watch waves lap at the shore, listen to the wind move through tree branches. And we need time to do nothing at all.

Are you smirking right now? Wondering who has time to stare into space and listen to the wind?

I'm quite serious. When was the last time you gave yourself time to notice without purpose? When was the simple and undistracted act of *being* your main activity? (And no, watching a video of a cat playing piano doesn't count.)

In fiction, poetry, and music, white space is used between scenes, images, and sound on purpose. The white space is a container for energetic reflection. It's there to give you a moment to digest what just happened. To let the last word or sound ring out for effect. It's an opportunity to pause, to make some sense of what has just finished, to get ready for what comes next. White space gives you permission to experience a moment in that moment.

As a writer, you value white space in your daily life for the same reasons. Empty time gives your mind the opportunity to process your thoughts, wonder about things you don't know yet, see connections, work through story problems.

It's difficult to access your creative curiosity, the state of mind you need for creative writing, if you haven't experienced any true blankness for a while. Do you have enough white space in your life? Can you give yourself more?

Take a moment now to give your mind time and space to digest what you've just read. Notice your surroundings, your breath, the sensations in your body.

This is white space in action.

Once you know how to incorporate white space into your routine, you can use it to invite creative curiosity. You'll start to recognize signs that your mind is ready to engage with your writing—perhaps a spark of an idea, a feeling of renewed energy, or simply a sense of calm focus. Whether you're about to begin writing or you're in need of a mindful break, the practice of creating white space will serve your creative process.

PRACTICE

Your creative mind needs a blank canvas. Here's an exercise that will train you to create that space.

1. Cancel something you'd planned. This can be a small thing, like doing the dishes before you go to bed. Or it can be more significant, like attending a meeting or a dinner party. When you cancel it, make it conscious: you are choosing to save your attention. Once you cancel something, you'll have created some white space in your life.

2. Now keep this new space empty. Watch what happens. Very likely, an event, opportunity, or demand will threaten to fill it up immediately. Be diligent! Do absolutely nothing with that piece of time. Don't even write.

3. What? Cancel something in order to do *nothing*? Yes. The goal of this exercise is to create space. That's it.

4. Set aside white space for a minimum of ten minutes a day, at least three days in a row. After doing nothing consistently for this short period of time, you'll notice a shift. White space gives your unconscious mind the power to

do its best work: it can process your thoughts and emotions for you, which helps you learn and grow from your experiences.

5. Pay attention to the subtle differences in your state of mind. After a week, you may start to feel more like yourself. Your sleep may improve, and you might even have an unusual dream—this is a sign that your imagination is awakening. Some people have flashes of memory or get a song in their head for no reason. This change is gradual and will depend on your life circumstances and mental habits.

6. Watch for moments of curiosity and track them. When you start to notice things you haven't noticed before, you know that you have made room for your creativity. *Your sweater is knitted from two strands of slightly different-coloured yarn. The top leaves of the poplar tree are trembling, but there's no breeze down where you're sitting.* Collect these moments in your bullet journal: make a simple list titled *Creative Curiosity.* By paying attention to the mental quality that accompanies their appearances, you'll build momentum. Soon, your creative curiosity will bring you new questions, patterns, interests, and ideas.

7. Continue to build white space into your daily routine. Your attention is a resource. Make the choice to save your attention and develop white space as a habit of consciousness. If you're a planner, schedule white space into your calendar. If you prefer to go with the flow, set an alarm on your phone to go off at a random time of day as a reminder to do nothing.

8. Refocus on your writing practice. Your white space has a synergistic relationship to your writing time. Empty time isn't idle. The benefits in your writing will come as a result of the space you've made for your creative curiosity. Revel in the gorgeous, abundant feeling that emerges as interesting ideas, images, and emotions arise more freely.

*

BEING WHOLE-MINDED

Finding words for our different states of consciousness is like finding names for paint colours. We use the word *butterscotch* to describe a certain creamy golden hue, and this works because it evokes a distinct colour, flavour, scent, and texture, and possibly even nostalgia and memories, all at the same time. Our body knows the complex, multi-sensory experience of butterscotch on many levels.

Our bodies know the multi-sensory experience of *flow*, too—the word evokes water, effortless movement, immersion, and a sense of that optimal performance associated with the flow state. When spoken, it embodies the experience, because the word itself has a smooth, flowing sound.

I wish there was a better word to evoke the delicious and complex experience of the whole-minded state. This is a state of integrated awareness where you can sense the internal signals from your body, like your heartbeat and breathing, at the same time as the signals coming from your external environment, like the smell of popcorn and the sound and vibration of a phone buzzing. (Is the word *holosentience*? *Panawakeness*?)

For creative writers, the ability to focus deeply is the key that unlocks the door to flow, that peak state of writing performance and enjoyment where your words seem to come effortlessly. Being whole-minded sets you up for better focus and it increases the likelihood of experiencing a flow state.

When we're in the whole-minded state, our brain takes all the information from inside and outside the body and puts it together to make sense of what's happening in the present moment. This helps us think more clearly, feel more vividly, and better understand whatever experience we're having. With this fuller picture, it's easier for us to pay attention to what we're doing. We can really focus with concentration and ignore distractions. When we're in this state, we're more likely to do our best work and *feel* like we're doing our best work, too.

PRACTICE

The following two practices—inner focus practice and whole-minded practice—are tools you can use separately or together to strengthen your overall ability to focus deeply.

Many of the writing practices in this book will ask you to notice your internal physical and/or emotional signals, so building your inner focus is a great foundational practice to get you primed to recognize those. Having a non-judgmental awareness of internal sensations is also key to being whole-minded; these two practices work together.

Start with the inner focus practice and follow it with the whole-minded practice. Together, they should take about twenty minutes.

Inner focus practice

Try recording these instructions on your phone, in your own voice. You can replay the audio whenever you want to practise.

1. Find a comfortable seated position and let yourself get settled. With your eyes open, take three deep breaths, in through your nose and out your mouth. With your third exhale, close your eyes.

2. Start to notice how your body feels. Feel your weight on the chair or the ground beneath you. Bring your awareness to the soles of your feet. Slowly move your awareness upward, and bring your attention to physical sensations as you do. Notice your toes, ankles, and legs. Are they tense or relaxed? Warm or cool? Move to your hips, lower back, and abdomen. Be aware of any areas of comfort or discomfort. Focus on your chest and upper back. Notice your heartbeat, if you can. Bring awareness to your shoulders, arms, and hands. Are they heavy or light? Loose or firm? Finally, focus on your neck, face, and scalp. Notice any tension or relaxation in these areas.

3. Now notice a specific physical sensation—maybe your hands in your lap—and focus on that sensation for the next few moments.

4. Now draw your focus to your breath. You're going to train your focus by placing it on the simplest thing: your breathing. Pay attention to each breath as it passes; focus on the sensations of breathing. You aren't forcing anything. You're just noticing your natural breathing. Maybe you feel the sensation of air moving in and out of your

nostrils. Maybe you feel your chest and abdomen expand and contract with each inhale and exhale. Wherever it's easiest for you to notice it, leave your attention there.

5. Notice that when you do this for a bit, your mind begins to wander. This is normal. The goal of this practice is just to notice when this happens. When it does, bring your attention back to your breath. This is the training.

6. Now begin counting your breaths. Count "one" on the inhale, "two" on the exhale, up to ten. Then start over. If you lose count or get distracted, simply start again at one. Continue this rhythmic counting, maintaining a gentle focus on your breath. If you notice your mind wandering away from your breath, gently smile at your mind and its thinking powers, and come back to notice your breath again, and start over. Continue this until you cycle through three sets of ten.

7. Turn your attention inward to your emotional state. What emotions are present? Where do you feel them in your body? If you notice any strong emotions, simply observe them without trying to change or judge them. See if you can locate where in your body you feel these emotions most strongly.

8. Slowly bring your awareness back to your breath. Take a few deep breaths, feeling the connection between your mind and body.

9. Gently open your eyes. Bring this heightened awareness with you into the next practice or the rest of your day.

Whole-minded practice

The whole-minded state is a condition of open, relaxed awareness where you're attuned to both your inner sensations and your external environment. It opens up your dilated vision, or what I like to call broad awareness: the calm, open gaze you have when you're aware of your entire visual field. This practice is particularly useful when you want to learn how to do something new, or when you feel creatively stuck, stressed about time, or need a break from intense focus (like reading or writing). While it might sound complex, being whole-minded is simpler than you might think. Here's one way to bring yourself there.

1. Look up and across the room to where the wall meets the ceiling. Keep your eyes raised but relaxed, without straining. Notice how your peripheral vision expands.

2. Hold up the first two fingers of each hand in front of you. Look through them, seeing both your fingers and the junction between the wall and ceiling.

3. Slowly move your hands away from each other. Continue until your hands are at the edges of your peripheral vision. Notice that you can still see your fingers while looking straight ahead.

4. Move your hands behind your head. Even though you can't see them, try to sense their presence.

5. Snap your fingers behind your head. Use this sound as a sensory cue to lock in this state of expanded awareness.

6. Take a moment to notice what you're experiencing. How has your perception changed? What do you notice about your surroundings that you didn't before?

Practice this exercise regularly to make entering the whole-minded state easier and more natural. With time, you'll be able to shift into this state of open awareness whenever you need to relax and/or open your mind to more possibilities.

*

PEACE

Creative curiosity emerges from a sense of peace and calm. You can practise recognizing and finding this state as part of your writing practice.

Research in psychology and neuroscience has shown us that creativity may be impossible to access when we are anxious. We cannot be both creative and anxious at once. Which means that when you learn how to calm your nervous system, it becomes possible for you to write creatively, generate new ideas, and use your imagination to its full potential.

Anxiety can spike when we anticipate future concerns. Simply not knowing what will happen next can trigger our anxiety. Interestingly, this same state of not knowing is where our most engaging writing often emerges: when you feel surprised by yourself, perhaps laughing out loud as you write an unexpected piece of dialogue.

How do you remain calm when you don't know what will happen next? The antidote to anxiety is presence: be here now.

That's easier said than done—anxious thinking is an unconscious behavioural pattern. It's hard to stop the anxiety cycle once it starts, kind of like the continual desire for the next crunchy hit of sodium that comes with eating salty snacks. Each anxious thought can bring up another anxious thought, until you're thinking a new anxious thought every few seconds, causing your body to respond with shallow breathing, muscle tension, or nausea.

You can interrupt this unconscious thought pattern by noticing the things your body can see, hear, smell, feel, or taste. In other words, use your writing practice to help you become aware of where you are right now. A list works well: write down fifteen concrete details that are here with you in the present moment.

A deep part of you is always unconsciously aware of the present moment. This part of yourself notices the qualities of things as they are right now and understands sensations of texture, sound, scent, taste, and colour. When you bring this part of yourself into your conscious awareness, you can find peace. Become a witness to your own five senses and watch your anxiety subside.

From a sense of peace, your creative curiosity can emerge. Creative curiosity loves to make something out of nothing. It tracks signals and clues, connects thoughts and ideas, and finds patterns in systems. Its gaze is neutral—it observes without judgment, simply noticing what is, without labelling it as good or bad. It sees the question "What will happen next?" as an adventure full of endless possibility. But before it can start creating, you need to find a sense of peace, even if it's only briefly. Here's how.

PRACTICE

This practice helps you interrupt your anxious thought cycle and allows your creative curiosity to emerge. It takes less than five minutes.

Find a space to sit with your writing notebook and pen.

Start by noticing a few sensory details around you. Direct your attention to things your body can see, hear, smell, feel, and taste. Write down:

- five colours you see right now

- four sounds you hear right now

- three textures you can feel with your skin right now

- two smells you can sense right now

- one thing you can taste right now

Once you cycle through all five senses, pause to notice your state. You should already feel more grounded and present. That's because your body and mind are working together, showing you where you are. You aren't in the future or in the past. You're here right now.

Reflect on the change you notice, to help deepen and anchor that sense of calm.

*

COMMIT WITH YOUR HEART

Deciding and committing are related but different actions.

You make a decision when you choose to do something, either instantly or after thinking through the various alternatives.

Committing, on the other hand, follows a decision. It involves dedicating yourself to the thing you've chosen to do, regardless of any obstacles or challenges that may arise. Commitment requires ongoing effort, courage, perseverance, and a willingness to prioritize the activities you want to pursue.

When we think about writing, we often frame it as a responsibility—something we should do or must do. But what if you approached it as play instead? Imagine the difference between making time for a chore versus making time for something you truly enjoy. This shift in perspective can transform how you relate to your writing practice. When I talk about making a commitment, I'm not talking about fulfilling an obligation but about creating space for your joy and self-expression. With this mindset, committing to your writing evolves naturally.

If you've made the decision to write, the next step is to commit to your writing. The rest will come more easily. You might be hesitating to fully commit because you know, deep down, that doing so will set off a series of changes in your life. But if you truly want to write, you need to take this next step. Commit to devoting time to your writing, even if you don't feel like you have enough room in your schedule, even if you're unsure about what you're going to write. Your commitment should stand firm even when you feel uncertain about what might happen with your writing—whether you'll find your voice, complete your projects, or how your work might be received.

Let your heart get involved in the promise. Start by imagining yourself writing for pleasure and fun. See if you can picture it in your mind or feel it in your body. Your arms are loose, your breathing is deep, and you feel light, moving with the flow of ideas and words. Close your eyes and focus until you can start to recognize those feelings in your body, right now.

Once you have physically welcomed those sensations, it can be easier to make a commitment to write. Make your commitment with love and integrity. A heartfelt promise charges your energy and unconscious motivation to write. It can also carry you through any moments of doubt and tension that arise as part of creative practice.

By committing with your heart, you're choosing to view your writing as a source of joy rather than an obligation. Notice how making time for pleasure feels different than making time for responsibility. This shift in perspective—from duty to delight—can transform your relationship with writing, making your commitment not just easier to keep, but a source of ongoing inspiration and fulfillment.

Now that you've made this heartfelt commitment, it's time to sculpt your days, your weeks, and your life into a new shape that includes writing. This is where the rubber meets the road—where your commitment transforms into action.

Your writing won't happen if you don't make time for it. I know that sounds obvious. But this is the most common barrier I see in the writers I work with. It's my own biggest challenge, too. So your next bold creative action is to carve out space in your life for writing. Depending on your schedule and the commitments you have already made, this can feel like carving out of foam, wood, or granite. Whatever the material, approach this with patience and persistence—whether you're making quick, easy cuts or chipping away bit by bit.

Work writing time into your schedule *after* you've made the heartfelt commitment to write. Otherwise, those time blocks may come to feel burdensome, and every time you look at your calendar, you'll feel a subtle sense of disappointment. This can quickly devolve into a loop of negative reinforcement.

To help you translate your commitment into a concrete plan, here's a practice that will guide you in sculpting your time.

PRACTICE

1. Make a list of all your current commitments. Consult your planner, online and physical calendars, and to-do apps so you don't miss anything. Consider your current commitments, responsibilities, day job, and relationships, and also

consider your physical life, social life, and spiritual life. How are you currently filling your time?

2. Once your list is complete, you can begin to sort and edit it. If you're a busy person with a full life, this may be bracing. Writing doesn't have to be your top priority, but to make time for writing, you'll need to stop doing at least some of the other things you're already doing.

3. Get ready to be decisive.

4. Assess your current commitments. Mark the ones that are truly non-negotiable. Your new schedule will include writing and these other priorities. The rest of the items on this list can change. You may need to allocate your time, money, and energy differently in order to give your writing the space it needs. Think of this as a creative action. This is where you begin to sculpt the material of your life.

5. Decide how much time you want to give your writing and establish a consistent cadence. Will you write once a day, three times a week, or for two hours every Sunday evening? Blocking off this time is the biggest shift you're going to make to your life. Once you do this, you'll re-sort the other priorities in your life out of necessity.

6. Decide on the length of your commitment. You need to pare back your non-writing commitments. At the same time, you don't need to make writing a priority at the expense of other activities in your life forever (unless you want to). Start by scaling back on a couple of other commitments for a fixed amount of time; one to three

months is a good time container to start with. Or consider committing for the length of one project.

Making a project-based or finite commitment to a writing practice is much easier to manage than making big, nebulous, life-altering schedule changes. When you choose your project and the length of your commitment, it makes it possible to schedule your writing, actually do it, and know when you've achieved what you set out to do.

Your project doesn't have to be a book. A project might also be three months of writing ten minutes a day, or something similar. The key is to make the project measurable so you can chart your progress and be convinced by your own accomplishments once you meet the end date.

7. Make cancellations. Cancel, pause, or reschedule some or all of the flexible appointments and dates that you've already made during your committed writing period.

8. Prepare to send more regrets. For the next few weeks, you'll have to say no to some things that might come up—dinner parties, a baby shower for that lovely woman at work, a coffee date with a friend you haven't seen for months.

9. You're going to write instead of doing these things. You can't do both—it's unreasonable to expect that from yourself. For the duration of your established time commitment, you'll get lots of practice saying, "No thank you."

10. You can set up a gentle autoresponder on your email to take the pressure off. Here's an example I've used in the past:

    Thanks for your email. I'm currently working on a project that needs my full attention, so I have reallocated my time from daily email management to focused writing until [date]. This means I'll be checking my email less frequently. I will read your email, but you can expect a slower response time. Please text or call me if your message is urgent. Thanks for your patience!

11. Keep life simple. That whoosh you feel after carving out the time to write? That's the feeling of cleared space and time with nothing in it. If you're a person who has been conditioned to live a full and busy life, white space may be an uncomfortable or frightening feeling.

12. Resist the urge to schedule major life events that conflict with your committed writing time. Don't plan a kitchen renovation, book a walking tour of Ireland, or adopt a new puppy—it may be tempting to think that you'll be able to write and do these things, once you've finished all the other cancelling and rescheduling. You won't.

13. Take a deep breath. Step into this time and space with active curiosity. You've made a heartfelt commitment to your writing, and now you've sculpted your time to honour that commitment. Now your writing practice can take root in the nice rich soil of your newly crafted schedule.

*

THE CHORDS ARE CONNECTED

One year for Christmas, my husband, Ryan, signed me up for piano lessons. It was a bold and loving gesture. I was excited and terrified by the gift because for years I had dreamed about one day learning how to play the piano. But I'd been too afraid to sign up for lessons myself.

They weren't easy, those first few Monday-afternoon lessons. I felt like a dolt—my fingers didn't work right and everything I played sounded childish and stunted. But after about five months of practising, I started to sound okay. I had perfected some chords, and I had learned how to build sets of chords called triads. The whole piano can be divided up into triads. I learned twenty-four of them—twelve major chords and twelve minor chords—that repeated in different positions on the keyboard.

One day, my teacher gave me an exercise. That night, I was to write down each of the twenty-four triads on small pieces of paper and put the papers in a jar. I'd pick four of them at random and put them in an ordered loop. Then I had to write a stanza. The following Monday, I was to play the loop of chords for her.

In other words, I had to write a song in one week.

After just five months of the most basic, kindergarten-level piano lessons, she wanted me to become a singer-songwriter? I did not feel ready for this. Far from it.

I balked at the first obstacle: pulling four random chords. Why did she want me to pick them at random? Wouldn't that sound terrible?

"All the chords are connected," she said. "They have relation-ships with each other. Your song will find the relationships."

I went home and did the assignment. I picked four chords at random. As I'd feared, they immediately sounded awful together. (I don't remember which chords I chose, but I do remember the grave look a musician friend gave me when I told him what they were.)

I worked at those chords for most of the week. I put them in different sequences, trying to find the least-horrible sound they could make together. I played them soft and loud, low and high, short and cute, and long and mournful. I tried to make them harmonize. I tried to make them fit. I tried to make them play nice.

After five days, something had changed. I had stopped hear-ing them as awful. The chords had just started to sound like... themselves. I was no longer playing them to figure out how they were supposed to go together or to make them do something they didn't want to do. I had started to listen to them. And as I paid attention to them, they taught me how to hear them.

That's when my assignment got interesting. It was as though each chord had a voice, and they were trying to have a conversation. I moved them around so they could hear each other better, so they could answer each other's questions. I realized that my piano teacher was right: the different chords were in a relationship, and the way I played them—the context I put them in—turned them into a kind of aural story.

By the end of the week, my whole state of mind had changed. I heard the four chords in my head, all day long; I was inside the song I was writing. The Vitamix motor revved in the same tune and the starlings outside were singing along with me. Once I stopped forcing the pieces together, I could see how they were already connected. Now the rest of the world was joining in and showing me how songs are made: through the chords' connections.

In one of my favourite essays by Zadie Smith, she writes about the creative process and how weird it feels to be in the middle of writing a novel and seeing connections everywhere around you. Magic happens, she says. Well, no—those are *my* words. She gives this phenomenon a much more rational name: "Middle-of-the-Novel Magical Thinking."

"The middle of a novel is a state of mind," she writes. "Strange things happen in it. Time collapses. I sit down to write at 9:00 a.m., I blink, the evening news is on and I've written four thousand words, more words than I wrote in three long months, a year ago. Something has changed. And it's not restricted to the house. If you go outside, everything—I mean, everything—flows freely into your novel. Someone on the bus says something—it's straight out of your novel. You open the paper—every single story in the paper is directly relevant to your novel."

Stories are written in the same way songs are made. The truth is, everything is connected. In our writing, we can be honest about what we hear, see, and feel. We try to be awake to it; we try to be true to life. We witness the chords of character and setting, and we listen for the connections between them. We feel the conversations.

Let's say you're writing a story about a character who finds lost things: a single gold hoop earring, a five-dollar bill, a stray tabby cat named Grivenstone. You don't know where that name came from—it's not a word you've heard before, not a name you've read anywhere. In your story, the man buys a used truck and finds a notebook filled with handwritten poems in the glovebox. Three days later, you take a trip to a foreign city thousands of kilometres from your home. On a walk in this new place, you see a discarded cardboard coffee cup. A stamped logo on it reads *Grivenstone Books & Café*. You feel a shiver down the back of your neck. You decide to visit this café, and after a few inquiries you find it on a side street. As your barista makes you a latte, a man with one gold hoop earring approaches the counter. "Some guy left this book of poetry in my car last night," he says, and sets the book on the counter. The cover reads *The Book of Lost Things*. You pay for your latte with a five-dollar bill. On the shelf behind the barista, a grey tabby cat blinks at you and flicks the tip of its tail.

When we write, we are attuned to the subtle qualities of harmony and dissonance in elements of life and language. That's how we recognize which details are connected and how to arrange them into narrative patterns.

It feels like magic when this phenomenon occurs in your own life. But later, when you recall the synchronicity, it might not still carry the same twinkling, electric charge. The paper coffee cup feels like a coincidence, taxi drivers probably find lost books in their cars all the time, tabby cats in bookstores aren't that rare, and the earring and the five-dollar bill? You'd probably see those every day if you were looking for them. Uncanny—but not much more than that.

This happens because when you're paying close attention to the connections you encounter, when you see how things exist in relationship to one another, you might enter a trance of connection—your mind sees the magic.

As I sat at the piano that Monday, my fingers found their way through the once-discordant chords. The melody that emerged wasn't sophisticated or particularly beautiful, but it was mine—it came from a week of listening carefully and allowing connections to form. My teacher nodded along, a small smile playing at the corners of her mouth. I felt a mix of pride and wonder; I had created a coherent song out of nothing, simply by paying attention. In the years since, I've carried this lesson into my writing. Just as those four random chords taught me to hear hidden harmonies, I now approach my stories with an open mind and attentive ear. I trust that the connections are there, waiting to be discovered.

PRACTICE

It doesn't matter if the sparks of synchronicity you encounter are explainable or not. What matters is that when you sense them, you understand them as a sign that you're on the right path. This is a signal that you're in a state of mind that is attuned to pattern, poetry, and connection—you're in the zone of creative curiosity.

Keep track of these moments in your bullet journal. Collect every insight and buzzy experience you notice and revisit your list often to remind yourself of the times you've found yourself on the right track, and to remember what it feels like to be entranced by your creative work.

As you record your list of notes and "aha" moments, you're telling your unconscious mind to keep looking for useful story elements all around you, and to align itself with what feels true. Later, when you hit an inevitable creative plateau or lose inspiration, this list will be a log for your creative curiosity. It's proof that magic is always accessible when you remain open to it.

＊

YOUR OTHER BRAIN

As writers, we often focus on the power of our minds, but there's another source of wisdom we shouldn't overlook: our gut. While it's become common knowledge that we have a complex neural network in our digestive system, what's less understood is how this "second brain" influences our creative process.

The web that lines your gut contains more than a hundred million neurons. Neuroscientists call this neuro-mass the enteric nervous system.

This system's job is far more complex than simply digesting the banana oat muffin you ate for breakfast. It's part of a complex brain-gut connection that also influences our emotions and physical sensations—like that swirl of butterflies in your stomach when you think about getting on a plane to meet that special someone in London.

Many of us are already used to thinking of our gut as the home for a kind of sixth sense. We describe our instincts as "gut feelings." When we want to make sure we're making a decision that is true to who we are, we talk about having a "gut check." As creative writers, we rely on our instincts and our senses to tell stories just as much as we rely on language.

Language is something that our brain is *really* good at. Up there, we have mastered the art of naming things. Our vocabularies of words and their meanings fit into the ordered structure of dictionaries like the pieces of a puzzle.

But to create art through story, scene, and character, we have to incorporate our gut, too. When we write from our gut, we channel our intuitive intelligence and transfer that experience to our readers. Writing with all of our instincts firing brings a deeper, multi-layered connectivity to our work.

Being a good writer is about more than mastering language. You want to use both brains—the one in your head and the one in your gut—when you're writing. You just want to use each of them in the right way.

Don't ask your brain to be your instinct.

If you rely solely on your brain, you might feel afraid and alarmed from overthinking. Instead, keep your head happy with a job to track—a word count, a writing formula that has steps, a collection of index cards with scenes you want to write, hours and minutes that you've written, or the number of insights you've had. Keeping your brain occupied with logic will give your gut brain the space it needs to feel and express itself.

Don't ask your gut to be your editor.

If you do, you'll give yourself a stomach ache. Syntax, grammar, and spelling are not what your gut cares about—it can't even read! Ask it to help you feel the foreboding shadows in a room. Ask it to show you what it feels like to be someone who is expecting a surprise birthday party. Ask it to describe a lemon tree, a mandolin solo, a man wearing red shoes, or the scent of smoked paprika. Don't rush it—enjoy the good feelings that flood your system and fully appreciate the unique sensation of writing with feeling and emotion.

Practise giving your brain and your gut the right kind of work to do, along with the space and time to work the way they each need to. They operate differently, and that's part of their beauty.

Our gut works best with lots of white space and clear swaths of "unproductive" time: that's how you can hear what your instinct is telling you. Take breaks, go out in nature, and spend time doing nothing each day. Rest makes success.

Our brain is eager to execute and complete tasks, put things into the right file folders, and do it all correctly. You'll want to enlist its powers for editing and revision when you're working on future and final drafts.

Sometimes you get a feeling—maybe you can see something in your story coming toward you in the form of an image, sound, or other sense. Maybe it's a chipped duck figurine, a hoarse laugh, or the tang of gasoline. Whatever it is, it wasn't there at first, until, suddenly, it appears. You didn't imagine it—you sensed it.

So you write it down. Then the most amazing thing happens:

You sense even *more* of the scene. And more. And more. Your attention to what you see and feel makes the story you are writing grow. It becomes real as you write it. This is your gut at work, mediated through the brain's language centres.

Try not to interfere with the natural ways your head and gut operate, but do let them collaborate. Use your brain to erect a boundary around your creative curiosity—your instincts, your gut. Then, as you pay more attention to your gut, as you actively embrace your inherent curiosity, more of your story will reveal itself to you.

*

EDNA-MIND AND VIOLET-MIND

Edna is the rational part of my mind, a dedicated leader who is smart about a lot of things, but she tends to hold forth and could benefit from more active listening. She's driven, dependable, and communicates with me directly. She talks over the subtle signals that come from the quiet, inquisitive part of my mind. That part of my mind has a deep sense of wonder, but it is so unassuming that I forgot to give her a name for many years. This is Violet.

Edna wants total power over what I write. She wants to be in charge of everything, including my first drafts. But if I follow her instructions exclusively, my story is predictable, unsubtle, full of clichés. She points out everything bad about my first draft as I write it, then she blames me when the writing isn't good. Sometimes when she's advising me, I freeze up and can't write at all.

Violet is soft-spoken, curious, and imaginative. She doesn't use words directly but communicates through images and emotions. When I follow Violet's instructions, my sentences glimmer with unusual connections, symbols, and metaphors. My handwriting loosens, I write over the margins, and I leave spelling and grammar errors littered all over the page. That's because Violet is more concerned with how something feels than how it's spelled.

This kind of writing doesn't make sense to Edna. It's messy and chaotic. If she's not busy keeping something else in order, Edna will notice Violet's signature moves right away. She will loudly and concisely let me know why it's really bad writing. It's a mess—she's often right. But there's magic in the mess! When it's time to sift through it, Edna's the one to help me make sense of it.

If I only listen to Edna, I miss out on the magic and beauty that Violet brings to my writing. If I only listen to Violet, my writing is incoherent and ineffective.

In a state of open, broad awareness—the whole-minded state—you experience an integrated consciousness of internal signals from your body and external cues from your environment. You may slip into this mindset naturally when visiting a bustling beach on a warm summer day: you're simultaneously aware of your own steady breathing and the gentle rhythm of your heartbeat and the crash of waves, the scent of salt and sunscreen, the warmth of sun on your skin, and the colourful umbrellas dotting the sand.

Just as we can integrate our awareness of internal and external stimuli, we can also cultivate a balance between the analytical and intuitive aspects of our mind. This is another facet of the whole-minded state: the harmonious integration of our inner Ednas and Violets.

One of the biggest challenges of our craft is developing the skill to harmonize these inner voices and cultivate a mindset where logic and imagination, and structure and creativity, can coexist and complement each other. The whole-minded state isn't about choosing one over the other, but rather integrating these two intelligent voices so they work together in harmony rather than in opposition. We want to give our personal Violets permission to take up more space and time, while letting our Ednas step back. We do our best writing when our inner Ednas and Violets dance together.

This whole-mindedness allows you to write with both analytical precision and creative intuition. To master this skill, it might be helpful to name the characters in your mind. This puts a bit of space between you and the thoughts in your head, so you can modulate their volume and power, to better balance your mind for writing.

Who is your Edna? Who understands the way sentences should go together, structures your timeline logically, and makes sure your arguments are coherent? Ednas insist on clarity and order, and ensure every detail is precise. They could show up as an explainer, a critic, or the grammar police. They're super-smart, but if they dominate your writing time, they can stifle your creativity. What would you name them?

Who is your Violet? Who's the curious observer who watches light play on the walls, notices the spiky flavour of spearmint gum in your mouth, and hears the fire crackle with warmth? They probably make their presence known to you without words, so you'll have to pay close attention to understand what they're showing you about space, colour, emotion, and character. Their advice brings depth and nuance to your scenes. They're full of wonder and imagination, but they can be easily overlooked or pushed aside by your Edna if you don't deliberately give them enough space and attention. What would you name them?

Once you establish a relationship with these two characters, you can voluntarily call them up and/or quiet them down. You want to write with both clarity and imagination, so you'll want to take their advice in different ways, at different times. Set good boundaries and treat them both with respect. By cultivating this writerly whole-mindedness, you're not only enhancing your creative process, but also deepening your overall practice of integrated awareness in all aspects of your life.

$*$

YOUR INNER PROTECTOR

Trying something new can prompt an internal response of doubt or criticism. This is a natural reaction to change; it's a human safety instinct that kicks in whenever we leave our comfort zone. Writers might be more familiar with it as the inner critic.

Even thinking about writing can cue this response: *You probably shouldn't start writing now... You don't have time anyway... There are so many books out there already... You're too old to start now... Even if you try, it's unlikely that you'll be successful.*

And when you do actually start writing something new, that inner voice will turn up the volume to get your attention, because you didn't heed its early warnings—you had the audacity to go for it anyway.

Say I'm writing an exploratory scene in the first draft of a new story. *Ugh, that sentence sucks.* I wince, scratch it out, and try another sentence, this time in the voice of a character I'm still getting to know. *No no no—you're terrible at dialogue. Don't bother finishing this story—your whole idea is boring.* That's my inner critic speaking at top volume, and the underlying message is always the same: *Stop writing.*

Why do I listen to that critical inner voice? Because I've learned to trust that same voice in other situations, where it has kept me safe from harm.

Your inner critic is trying to protect you. It belongs to the part of your mind that's always on guard to protect you from dangerous situations. Humans are naturally wired to pay attention to it, because when we try new things, they often feel like a threat to our sense of comfort. When you're writing with creative curiosity, you're trying new things and taking risks, and that can cause your mind to freak out.

This protective instinct serves you well in other areas of life. It's the same voice that warns you when you're about to step off a curb without looking both ways. That quick internal *Watch out!* has likely saved you from walking into traffic more than once. Or maybe it's the voice that tells you to double-check the stove before leaving the house, preventing a potential disaster. In these situations, heeding your cautionary inner voice is crucial for your safety.

It wants you to be well. It's on your side. But when you go into your curious, playful, emotional, and non-verbal zone, it doesn't understand what you're doing. It thinks maybe you've gone off course. Possibly even into danger. *Stop right there! You don't know where that sentence will lead you!*

The arguments put forward by your interior voice can sound convincing. The trick is to remember that they stem from the very human impulse to stay in your comfort zone. But you have control: you can learn how to recognize that voice for what it is, and you can decide to take creative risks anyway.

In *Writing Down the Bones*, author and writing teacher Natalie Goldberg refers to our internal voices of self-doubt and criticism as "guardians at the gate." I picture these guardians as two fierce, protective lions with golden, sun-warmed coats and swishing tails, crouched on either side of the entrance to a long, tree-lined driveway. Their amber eyes track my movements, and I can almost hear their steady breathing. At the end of the driveway is a beautiful villa that contains the richness of the story I'm writing and all the creative energy I need to write it. Getting into that villa means recognizing the presence of these living, breathing lions, understanding how they serve as my inner protectors, and finding the courage to walk past them. My strategy is to admire their beauty and thank them for their presence—when I do this, their muscles relax, and they do not attack me.

You don't have to silence your inner critic before you start writing. You don't need to feel sure about success before you pick up a pen and notebook. Writing a book doesn't require confidence; it asks you to acknowledge your inner critic, to learn how to live with self-doubt, and put pen to paper anyway.

How do you finish a first draft when the opinionated voice in your head keeps interrupting you with unsolicited advice? Respond to your inner critic as if it is separate from the rest of you by giving it some attention. In other words, let it know you're listening to it.

Getting angry and fighting with your inner critic may feel like an empowered response, but it doesn't actually work well.

Why? Because your critic will dig in its heels even more—it doesn't see that you're taking it seriously. Instead, learn how to recognize its voice, practise listening to it neutrally, and redirect its energy into creation rather than stagnation.

The goal of the following exercise is to help you do this.

PRACTICE

1. On a page in your bullet journal, write down all the things your inner critic tells you about your writing. Write down the things you fear the most. It's okay to get into dark stuff here. Jot it all down.

2. Now ask yourself: *Who does this voice belong to?* Imagine the physical embodiment of your inner critic's voice. Is it a human character, an animal, or a mythic/imaginary creature? Picture this character in your mind. Give it physical characteristics—eyes, wings, hands, teeth. Give this character a name.

3. Draw a simple picture of this character on a separate page. This drawing doesn't have to be a piece of art. Even an outline sketch is great. You can doodle in the details you imagined above. Write its name above its picture.

4. Write some of the worst phrases and opinions you collected in Step 1 all around the drawing. Draw little speech bubbles around the words so you can see it saying those things to you.

5. Look at the cartoon sketch on the page in front of you. You've taken those critical thoughts outside yourself

and now you can see them with perspective. They aren't true—they're thoughts that this weird figure thinks. It looks kind of cute, actually. Can you see that it's saying those things to you because you've started to take creative risks?

6. Go drink a glass of water or take a short walk to clear your mind. Come back to your desk and start writing. And when your inner critic protests, you can calmly respond: *Thank you, [name of your character], for paying attention. I am trying something new right now, and I know that's out of your comfort zone! It's okay. I am safe. You're so good at watching out for me. Can you please keep an eye on the time and tell me when thirty minutes of writing has passed?*

See how it feels in your body when you ask that part of your mind to be on guard for you.

The inner critic transforms into the inner protector through the process of acknowledgement and respect. Once you make peace with your inner critic, a quiet space can emerge, blank as a fresh white page. This is the time to begin your writing practice. Your inner protector, no longer a harsh critic but a loyal guide, can now help you maintain healthy boundaries. Tell it to monitor your energy levels and to signal when you need a break. Ask it to let you know if you're veering off track from your creative goals. Listen to it not as a command to stop but as a reminder to check in with yourself and your writing process.

WRITING IS A TRANCE

Imagine a flower garden blooming in full summer.

Pink roses tumble over the garden fence. Beside you, tall purple flowers grow on long stalks with rounded leaves. A lazy bumblebee bumps into their petals. The bee's buzz is a soft drone in the quiet, warm air. A puffy white cloud moves in front of the sun, and the air turns cool against your shoulders.

Whenever you imagine something, you can put yourself into a light trance. Even closing your eyes to remember something that happened last week can bring you under a slight spell.

Creative writing can also put you into a light trance, whether you're reading or writing.

There may be times when the act of writing pulls you into an even deeper trance state. For example, notice if you get sleepy as you're writing a scene. This is not because you're bored— it's because your brainwaves have slowed down in order to carefully imagine the details in the scene you're writing.

When you're thinking, solving problems, or processing information, your brainwaves are moving at a fast pace. And if you can ease off intellectualizing, you have the opportunity to heighten your imagination and concentration. You relax and become focused enough to imagine sensory details as you write them, like the warm, buttery scent of chocolate chip cookies when they come out of the oven.

When you continue relaxing your mind and slowing your brainwaves even more, your visualizations become increasingly vivid. This is where profound ideas live, in the realm of your deep, creative unconscious. These slower brainwaves are also associated with sleep and dreaming, and in this deeply relaxed state you may experience downloads of insight, connections, and ideas.

This deep trance state is my favourite for creative writing. I find daydreaming to be an incredibly productive way to spend my writing time. Get to know your own brainwaves and how you feel in different states of relaxation. Practise moving from stimulated thinking into relaxed awareness and back again, just to get the knack of moving back and forth. When you're searching for insight or new ideas, give yourself permission to close your eyes, to take a deep breath, to stop thinking and start daydreaming.

WRITE BY HAND

There's nothing inherently wrong about typing out a first draft, but I want to encourage you to write by hand.

Writing by hand can be a drag, I know. It feels less productive: it's messier, it takes longer, and it adds an extra step to the process, because at some point you have to transcribe what you've written on paper. A whole page of handwriting only equals about a half-page of typing, and an hour's worth of scribbling on a page can be unclear: those loops of ink don't evoke the same sense of finality or polish as a double-spaced page set in Times New Roman.

And yet.

Writing by hand is a powerful way to interrupt your usual thought patterns and work with your creative curiosity. The act of engaging with each letter, word, and sentence on a slow, imperfect, ink-to-paper level can change the writing experience entirely.

Handwriting is quality time. It creates the condition for your active mind to slow down because your mind has to move at your hand's pace. Your body becomes a key part of your work. True, you probably won't produce as many pages per hour by handwriting as you would if you were typing them. But that's not the point. The point of writing by hand is to train yourself to become more receptive.

As you write, you're working with energy. You want to be aware of subtle variables in energy because your awareness brings insight. There are important nuances within your creative process that are easy to miss when you're writing in a digital document. For example, the pressure and slant of your handwriting can tell you something about your emotional state. There are distinct curls I make in my lowercase letters that I've learned are a signal that I'm feeling playful—a sign that my curiosity is active. When my letters are more angular and the slant of my writing is uneven, I can tell that I'm unsettled. These physical cues prompt me to pause, ground myself, and shift myself into the whole-minded state before I continue. Writing by hand keeps the lines of communication open between your body and your mind. As you spend more time with your handwriting, you'll learn how to understand these signals better.

The brain perceives writing by hand as making art. When you use your hand to make a mark on a blank page, you're saying to your mind: *Now we are creating something.*

The impulse to solve a problem is different than the impulse to create something new—and it is in this subtle shift that the magic happens.

When you write the letter K with your pen, you are also drawing a picture of the letter K. Using your body to make this mark on paper activates the creative parts of your brain. These are the parts that understand the world through sensory detail. As you write by hand, your letters become words and sentences that communicate intellectual ideas. Your letters are also line drawings that go beyond language: they hold the contours of sensation and emotion.

When you create a story out of nothingness, when you paint pictures with your sentences, when you write characters who live and breathe as though they're real people, you're using your imagination. You can feel the difference.

The next time you write, try writing slowly. Forget about whole words for a moment and spend time with every single letter you write. Notice how your body feels after five minutes of this writing-drawing.

Don't underestimate the creative force that lives in your own handwriting. Writing by hand invites us to change our state of mind.

When you write by hand to describe the gentle rustle of leaves outside the kitchen window, notice if your experience of writing comes alive with extra energy. Physically slowing down gives you time to sense images more wholly on multiple levels. A yellow buttercup, wilted, rests on a table. A child blinks, eyelashes so long they touch his upper cheek. The sound of a metallic click comes from deep within a wooden trunk. You don't have to know what any of these details mean. You only have to write them down. Surprise and clarity arrive at once when you pay attention to creative curiosity.

Write by hand so you can do more than just jot down details. Write by hand so you can *become* the details.

Being curious means you don't know what comes next; paying attention requires you to explore the unknown. Writing by hand can make you feel impatient and jittery because your ego doesn't want you to explore unknown territory. Typing can be a way to escape your ego—if you type quickly enough, maybe you can outrun your inner critic.

But there is another, deeper benefit to slowing down—it helps you face your resistance. This builds your resilience to doubt and fear, and it strengthens your long term relationship with creative curiosity.

When you press Delete on the computer, you erase your tender ideas before they have a chance to take root. When the deleted sentence disappears from the page, it can also disappear from your consciousness.

In a first draft, you're not supposed to know if what you're writing is any good or not. You simply don't have access to critical analysis at this stage. Remember—curiosity is neutral. It observes without judgment, allowing you to explore ideas and possibilities without the constraints of preconceived notions of good or bad. Handwriting allows this to happen more readily.

Writing by hand creates a map of your explorations. Even if you cross out a sentence, the remains of that sentence are still there on the page. Their presence affects the next sentence you write, and the sentences after that. These unused sentences are markers for your subconscious. They are part of your material and cues for your next steps. Taking them away makes your creative work harder than it has to be.

One of the writers in my writing school made the switch from typing to what she now calls "slow writing"—she wrote the first draft of her novel by hand and transcribed each scene into her computer as she went. Handwriting created space for her unconscious mind to make more intricate connections, so her scenes arrived nuanced and whole.

As she transcribed each piece, she also revised it with care and attention. So that at the end of the process, the first draft she printed from her computer was actually a second draft. She said she thought the process of writing a novel by hand was going to take twice as long, but when she read her printout, she realized her scenes were already clear and interesting, and she had saved herself hours of revisions.

There are so many creative benefits to writing by hand. Ultimately, though, doing so is just another tool. See if it's useful for you. Every writer is different. If you already feel that combination of surprise and clarity as you type, great. No need to break something that doesn't need fixing. But if you're in a rut, or struggling to find perspective, you might be surprised at how much writing by hand can turn things around.

*

THE FRIENDSHIP EFFECT

Consider the last time you wrote a letter to a friend.

One morning, your friend Grant pops up in your mind. You haven't connected with him for a while. You have free time at lunch, so you write him an email to catch up. You start by saying hello and then tell him about the new project you're working on, and recount a funny story about your kid's recital. With a sense of ease and clarity you haven't felt for a long time, you share your thoughts about how taking time off work has made a profound difference to your health. The words spill out of you. You lose track of time until the clock catches your eye and you realize that forty-five minutes have passed.

You and Erin used to live across the street from each other, but she moved to another country and now the time difference makes phone calls difficult to organize. You think of her often, but you've become so busy that you missed her birthday this year. So you take time to buy her a cute card from your favourite indie bookshop. You include belated birthday wishes and some news of the day. You fill up both sides of the card and then write on the back of it. You reach the bottom of the card but you're in the middle of a story, so you grab a piece of paper and you keep writing. You feel focused and connected, the way you do when you're talking to Erin—so you grab another piece of paper and keep going until your message feels complete.

When you write a letter, you picture the person you're addressing and write with the intention and desire to connect. You don't worry about the literary quality of your sentences (although it feels good to craft them to sound just right, and you might even enjoy pausing to reread them yourself).

Letter-writing invites ease, grace, and humour. Your voice—freed from expectation, ego, and fear of failure—rings true. When you write a letter to your friend, your writing is spontaneous, authentic, and low-pressure. You do it because you want to feel the joy of connecting, sharing, and being yourself. Being present and joyful gives you energy.

But when it's time to work on your book, writing can suddenly feel so grim. You might have to trick yourself just to stay in the chair, at your desk. You may, perhaps, bribe yourself with things that bring you pleasure: a bowl of pretzels, chocolate almonds, a pour of Glenfiddich.

Why is writing so hard all of a sudden?

Writing a book feels hard because it's driven by external factors. You might feel pressure to write something that will meet the high standards of a future editor. You want the validation that comes from publication. These desires disconnect you from your true self and unplug you from your creative source.

But remember: writing is a form of presence and connection, a gift of quality time and attention that you're giving to someone else. The pleasure can be similar to what you feel when you decorate a birthday cake or send a care package to someone you love.

Your presence has value. When you give it to someone else, it's a gift. There's no goal—you're not trying to get anything out of it. Presence is the energy that lights up your writing.

Whatever energy you bring to your healthiest relationships you can also bring to the page. Your best writing isn't about upstaging, pretension, or trying too hard. It's about you being you and putting yourself on the page honestly.

So how do you write unapologetically and use your real voice in all of your writing projects, from birthday cards to books, when you also want your writing to garner external approval and success? Connect to the relational power of writing. Approach your book as if you're writing a letter to a dear friend who's genuinely interested in what you have to say.

By combining the slow, deliberate practice of handwriting with the authentic, connective energy of letter-writing, you can transform your writing experience. You'll find yourself more present, more creative, and more genuinely you on the page.

PRACTICE

This exercise helps you practise the mindset of letter writing so you can bring it into your own work. This takes a bit of repetition before it becomes a habit—but when you do it consistently, you just might change the way you think and feel about writing.

1. Make a decision to cultivate feelings of calmness, curiosity, and kindness. Your thoughts create your feelings, and feelings are based in neurochemistry. Instead of focusing on resistance, choose to write in the presence of other positive emotions.

2. Choose a writing space. This can be anywhere you would voluntarily choose to go if you were going to mindfully write a letter to a friend, like a café, your kitchen table, or on your lap at the train station. Do choose your writing space on purpose and, if necessary, clear clutter and eliminate distraction. You don't need a perfect writing desk: your focus and intention are what make a space special.

3. Close your eyes and imagine a friend listening to you with sensitive awareness. See the expression on their face, hear their voice as they laugh or say supportive words, and feel the quality of their energy when they give you the gift of their attention. What happens in your body? You may feel open and generous, or feel lightness or a glimmer of excitement. Let yourself hang out here for a minute. This is how you want to feel while writing.

4. Now think about something in your life that brings you happiness. It could be a beloved pet, a thought about nature, or a mug of your favourite tea. Start with a small feeling of appreciation and swirl it around your mind and your body. Inhale deeply and exhale slowly. Notice that as you focus on appreciation, the feeling grows. Let it grow bigger.

5. With these feelings alive in your mind and body, pre-
    pare to write by hand, in your notebook. Start with this
    prompt: "What I want to write about is..." Freewrite for
    up to ten minutes.

6. Afterwards, take a pause to check in: How relaxed do you
    feel? How easy did writing feel? How does it feel to let
    your writing bring out the best in you?

Remember, the goal is to approach your writing with the
same ease, authenticity, and connection you bring to writing
a letter to a dear friend. Practise this regularly, and you'll find
yourself naturally bringing this mindset to all your writing
projects.

*

FACE THE SHADOW

All stories are about change. If you ever reach a point in your writing where the action grinds to a halt, there is a very good chance that your characters need to do some shadow work.

The shadow is the opposite of the persona, which is the side of us that typically faces the world. Working with the shadow means looking directly at our most vulnerable parts, the aspects of who we are that we keep shielded, out of public view. Most often, we keep these parts hidden because they bring up feelings of shame. Psychologists also refer to these as our "disowned" parts.

In a story, shadows can be presented as a character's fatal flaws, buried memories, hidden motivations, feelings, or desires. Understanding shadow elements can be crucial to a story because they are directly related to a character's arc of change. Shadows organize the plot because they secretly control your character's actions (or non-actions).

Why do our characters so often fail to face their shadows? It's human nature to avoid shadow work, but here's another way to illustrate the answer to that question. As your central character drives your narrative forward, their burning desire or goal provides motivation and direction for the plot. Think of a character you are working with. What do they want? What is their goal?

In contrast, what is it that your character actually needs? What is the shift in perspective or environment that would bring them peace? For example, their goal may be to achieve fame as the world's first professional cloud sculptor, but what they really need is to release their grip on permanence and embrace the fleeting beauty of their art.

Open your bullet journal to a fresh page. On the left side of the page, write your character's goal. On the right side of the page, write what your character really needs. Now draw a vertical line down the page, separating the left and right sides. On the far left, near the top, sketch a simple sun. Imagine this line represents a brick wall on a sunny day. On the right side of the line, use your pen or pencil to lightly shade the area, representing the shadow cast by the wall. This shaded area symbolizes what your character needs but can't see. All they can see is what they want, represented by the sun on the left side.

Unseen shadows make for great story development. A character who goes after what he wants can create a lot of dramatic action, especially if it takes him in the opposite direction of what he needs. (This is a great structure for a romance.) And a character going after the same thing she wants in different ways, taking more risks as she goes, can build story pressure. (This is a great structure for a thriller.) At some point, though, if you don't start to chip away at that brick wall and let your character see their own shadow, the story can stall.

But as soon as your character finally sees the unseen and realizes that the shiny thing they've been chasing isn't the only option, they gain new perspective. This creates the conditions for transformation. It can also allow you to crack open a story that feels stuck.

We can help our characters see their shadow by first facing our own. Once we know how to navigate the slippery process of revealing and acknowledging our own disowned parts, we can use our experience in a story. Without shining light on our shadow, there can be no change for our characters—or for ourselves.

Of course, facing our shadow can be profoundly uncomfortable. We often distance ourselves from certain aspects of the characters we write for the same reason.

You can start here.

PRACTICE

Pick one of the following prompts, set a timer for ten minutes, and respond to the prompt by hand in your bullet journal.

If these questions make you cringe, that's the point. They're designed to make us squirm. Writing through the discomfort can lead to interesting discoveries. These may bring new insights and create the conditions for our own change and growth.

1. a) The thing I'm most afraid someone could say about my writing is...

   b) What is something I can do to expose myself to this fear in a safe way?

2. a) My character's worst personality flaw is...

   b) I share this personality trait because...

3. a) Who makes me envious? Why? What does that person have that I don't?

   b) How can I work toward giving myself what that person has that makes me jealous?

Pace yourself. You can spread this exercise out over a few weeks. Jot the rest of the questions down in your bullet journal and see which ones speak to you before you start writing. The goal is to make a connection between your conscious and unconscious minds, so pay attention to what you feel as you reflect on the questions. Notice where energy shows up in your body. Give yourself time to integrate after your writing sessions. Shadow work is not for the faint of heart, and it's not meant to be rushed. At the end of a shadow-focused writing session, release any charged energy by going for a walk, playing a song you love and dancing it out, or calling a friend.

The more you connect to your unconscious mind, the more it may reward you with significant dreams, restored energy, feelings of joy and relief, clarity and understanding, and better connections with the people in your life. Deep connections enhance your creativity: your stories become more nuanced, your characters come to life, and your writing flows more naturally. Doing shadow work not only makes you a better writer, but it also can make you a more balanced and content version of yourself.

*

CREATIVE CHALLENGES

Three of my writing students came to me separately for advice. Kayleigh was tired: she could see all of the flaws in her stories, but once she edited them, all she saw was more flaws. She wondered if she would ever feel like her writing was good enough.

Jas was revising pieces that she felt good about, and submitting them to journals and magazines, but she only ever received rejection letters. Would her writing ever be published?

Mateo had been dedicated to a project for some time but was having a hard time putting all of the writing together in a unified form. He felt that his writing was skilful but he couldn't seem to finish anything.

I knew exactly how they each felt. There were years when I wondered if I was ever going to finish my first book. I used to tell myself, *Even if you never publish this book, you are still a valid human being.* (Seriously!) And when I confessed this to an author I admired, she told me she felt the same way, only her mantra was *Even if I never publish another book, I am still a valid human being.*

Later, when I was struggling to write and revise my second book, her words echoed in my mind. That's when I really understood that being a writer is more than just writing books. Being a writer means challenging your spirit.

Being a writer means choosing to leave your comfort zone in pursuit of the unknown, to make yourself vulnerable over and over again. It's agreeing to experience change without being in control of how change happens. It's learning how to face your deepest fears and unresolved questions about life. And it's a willingness to do all of this on your own, with no promise that you'll achieve your desired outcome.

Writing books is an adventure for the human soul.

This is what I said to Kayleigh, Jas, and Mateo: Would it be okay if you loved the challenge? Or, at the very least, can you accept that these challenges are going to continue? Because they're not going to go away. The struggles you have right now are part of the journey. These aren't problems to solve or flaws to fix: they are features of the adventure you've chosen.

Being a writer is a lifelong process of discovery, and our writing flourishes when we give it time and energy, and approach it with curiosity. Overly high expectations and a constant state of yearning for results can create a perpetual cycle of desire and disappointment. This casts a spell of dissatisfaction: we then feel sad and stressed out, which drains the power from our creative curiosity.

We can break that spell by appreciating our creative challenges as opportunities for growth.

This process of change and integration is just as much your work as a writer as is writing itself. When you keep this in mind, being a writer becomes a much more interesting proposition, and every phase of your development offers fulfillment.

When I wrote the stories in my first book, I continually felt like I was trying and failing and trying again and failing again. When I wrote my second book, I came to understand that the process of writing books itself is trial and error. I felt the same way about this book as I was writing it!

I don't think there is any way to write a book without feeling a sense of struggle at times. Whether you're faced with a negative thought or feel caught in a frustrating spell of not achieving enough, see if replacing your dissatisfied thinking with appreciation and curiosity can break the pattern: *I appreciate that I am trying something new. I wonder how I will grow and change because of this creative challenge.*

*

AN EVEN BETTER IDEA

New ideas are delicious—and tricky.

Sometimes they feel like a gift: those first forsythia branches in spring that offer a burst of yellow so bright against the grey that you can hardly believe they're real.

Sometimes ideas come to interrupt our focus. They test our commitment to our main project by trying to persuade us with their cleverness.

When you make a commitment to finish writing a project, you're inviting magic to happen. The process will require endurance and resilience because stories inevitably include conflict, change, and complexity. At some point, on the way to its resolution, your story will ask you to describe a situation from an uncomfortable angle or to tell the truth about something you might be afraid to see.

Writing uncomfortable parts of a story can result in feeling uncomfortable. It can also raise thoughts like:

I don't know what I'm doing.

This doesn't make any sense.

I'm bored by my own writing.

Nobody wants to read this.

I have an even better idea!

You can honour the new idea without breaking your commitment to your current project. If a new idea comes while you're writing something else, acknowledge it by briefly pausing to note it. Write down the new idea in your bullet journal. Create a new folder on your phone or your computer or make one at your desk. Label this folder *Delicious New Ideas*. Put your idea into the folder.

Then keep your promise to the book you're still writing.

Boredom is a clue that you're avoiding your own emotional experience. What are you feeling under the boredom? What wants to be expressed?

Frustration, anger, or fatigue is a clue that you're resisting an uncomfortable or complicated issue in your writing or fighting against a revision you need to make.

If you're feeling alienated from your current project, you can ask it for help. Write to your creative unconscious in your bullet journal. Use the following practice as guide.

PRACTICE

This will help you reconnect with your current project when you're feeling alienated or tempted by new ideas.

1. Find a quiet moment. The ideal time to write to your creative unconscious is before you go to sleep or first thing in the morning. Have your bullet journal and pen ready.

2. Write to your creative unconscious using the following template (feel free to adapt this to your own voice): *There is another idea that wants my attention, and it's pretty exciting, but I want to keep going with our current project. I am curious about what we started, and I want to see what happens when we finish it. I know I made a commitment, but it's harder than I thought. Can you give me more energy? I promise to go out of my comfort zone in order to write this. Please move closer so I can see/hear/feel you. Do you have any advice for me? In order for me to write this, what do you need from me?*

3. After writing, close your journal and allow yourself to sleep or start your day.

4. Pay attention to what arises after you ask your creative mind for advice. Try to remember your dreams by writing them down in the morning. Notice the thoughts, symbols, and memories that come to you throughout the day. These are the answers to your questions.

5. Make time to record these observations in your bullet journal over the next few days.

6. Review your notes. As you become more familiar with this dialogue between your conscious and creative unconscious mind, you'll receive more insights and be able to recognize them more readily.

Writing is alchemy. When you write, you activate a process of change. As you write your story, your story is also writing you.

Let your story bring you into understanding.

Let your commitment to your story bring you through transformation.

*

REHEARSAL

In my teaching career, I've met many people who declare that writing exercises are a waste of time. To some extent, I get what they're saying: we're conditioned to measure our productivity in terms of what we can sell, and to use our time to maximize profit like workers at a factory. When some people sit down to write, they want to produce something that will be publishable. "I don't have a lot of time," they say. "If I'm going to write, I'm not going to faff around. I need to channel all my energy into the finished piece."

But we're *creative* writers—we aren't crunching data reports. Think about the way dancers or musicians interact with their art. The performance, the finished piece, is the culmination of hours of practice: boring warm-ups, weird experiments, and repetitive rehearsals. They show up to practice because that time is integral to the quality of their final performance.

Writing exercises are not a waste of time: you're an artist, and this is your practice.

It's worth taking the time to power up your state of mind.

Try easing into using language with ten or twenty minutes of loose, no-pressure writing in your freewriting notebook before you turn to your work in progress. Invite the part of your awareness that notices connections, colours, and feelings to work with the part that understands sequence and strategy. This activates your creative curiosity. And when you write with creative curiosity, you're activating your entire cognitive capacity—you bring your whole mind online. You can create an anchor for your writing practice by exclusively using a special notebook for exercises that aren't related to your current project. This notebook is like a painter's sketchbook: it gives you permission to explore and experiment. This can not only help you grow as a writer, but it can also aid you in bringing your best self to your work. You show up limber, flexible, and ready to write from a whole-minded state.

Your story is important. Finishing your book is important. But neither encapsulates everything there is to being a writer. Your finished work may be the performance piece of your writing life, but there is so much more to writing than the finished piece.

It doesn't matter whether you're just starting to learn about your voice and style, writing and publishing stories that will go in your first book, or working on your fourth novel: you need to make time for practice.

Writing practice and warming up might feel unproductive. Maybe there's a voice in your head that tells you that writing exercises are counterproductive. Notice if there is an urgency to this message—is it laced with anxiety about time? If so, then you know it's trying to motivate you with fear. Fear and creative curiosity don't coexist. Turn your motivation around by taking a few minutes to practise a small writing exercise. This can calm the anxious part of your mind. Notice what happens to the quality of your work once your brain feels more harmonized.

Writing practice isn't going to check anything off your to-do list. But the point of writing is to engage in noticing, make connections, and express insights through words—and this engagement happens just as much in exercises as it does in your work in progress.

Practice can also show you how to recognize your resistance. This is crucial, because if you don't recognize resistance for what it is, then you might only be able to write in fits and starts. You'll end up wondering why you aren't writing more regularly, or you'll force yourself and suffer as you write without joy and curiosity—this is an inefficient and suboptimal method, to say the least. Warming up teaches you how to reach your peak creative state more regularly. It gives you opportunities to note what you're learning through your practice and to become more flexible and more aware of your own creative process.

You build up your tolerance for writing by doing repetitions. This is just like lifting weights; with practice, you can progressively lift heavier weights over time. You learn what it feels like to push your limits. It's the same with writing: as you practise, you'll write more interesting, more complex scenes. And by doing this over and over again, you'll develop a writer's muscle memory. Doing reps helps you distinguish between the burn of intense and vibrant descriptions that challenge you and the ease of glossy stereotypes and clichés that barely exercise your creativity.

As you practise, you'll learn things about your characters, your sentences, and your stories that you didn't expect. You'll expand your capacity for surprise and delight in your creative life. Through consistent practice, you'll push past creative plateaus to take your writing to new heights. You'll discover depths in your work you never knew existed. This journey of continuous growth and exploration is how you truly discover who you are as a writer.

*

WRITE THROUGH UNCERTAINTY

Our writing practice can give us a chance to write without judgment. A daily warm-up routine—such as writing for ten minutes, responding to prompts, or morning pages—is akin to an athlete stretching before a game or a singer vocalizing before a performance. These practices are necessary and fundamental, a way to love and care for your craft.

After spending some time writing in shorter sprints, you might begin to desire more from your writing. You want to work with characters, setting, and story. You want to go deeper, follow through, and engage in a bigger project. You want to experience a character's transformation. You want to write a book.

Short, timed writing exercises are wonderful because they encourage and inspire spontaneity. But once you decide to write a story, or an essay, or a book, your writing practice becomes a bit more complex. Writing a book requires reflection.

Longer pieces of writing will ask you to be aware of your thoughts, insights, doubts, and desires, without letting them block your writing process. But you still need to be present when you're writing.

To do this, you're going to learn how to think and not think at the same time. Novelists live within this paradox every day and use a variety of approaches to dance with this challenge. The puzzle is figuring out how to remain unselfconscious while writing and stay open to conscious thought at the same time. This is where understanding your state of mind becomes part of your art.

Your writing needs your imagination. Your imagination wants to explore the unknown. But your mind is scared of the unknown—it can't help it. Your mind wants you to write something it understands already. But if you wrote something you knew already, then you'd be writing a report, not a story.

Your story is asking you to remain curious about what you discover as you explore the unknown. When you stay curious while writing, even when your mind tells you it might not be safe outside your comfort zone, you'll be able to explore the unfamiliar territory of your subconscious.

To write a story that invokes transformation, you may need to stay in the viscerally uncomfortable place of writing while simultaneously accepting the following truths:

Even if you're a plotter who outlines your entire story, you can't know for sure how all the details will unfold as you write.

You can't know for sure if you'll be able to finish it.

You can't know for sure if it'll be any good or not.

At first, embracing all of this uncertainty probably won't feel good. It won't feel like that fresh burst that comes from free-writing about a daily prompt for an allotted period of time. It won't feel like you're doing it right.

The process of creative writing is so mysterious and non-linear and weird that it can feel as though you're being asked to strap spoons on your feet, walk backwards, and fly—while holding peonies behind your back and eating a bowl of soup at the same time. Doing all that for more than ten minutes at a time? Impossible!

Stay in it. Cross your fingers and strap those spoons onto your feet.

What you're writing might feel like it's not making any sense. It might not feel like you're making anything good. It might not even feel possible to keep going sometimes. The structure of your story may not be recognizable to you until after you write it.

If you get some of those squirmy internal feelings of fear and uncertainty, let yourself be curious about them, too. This is where you need to remind yourself to stay in the process. Ask your fear what it wants you to know and write out the answers in your journal. Once your inner protector knows you've heard its warning, you may find that it settles and disappears.

The adventure can still get gnarly, though, even when you're listening to your true nature. Clues that you're writing with creative curiosity: You feel like you're doing it wrong. You feel out of your depth. After you write a fresh, fun part, the sparkly feeling wanes. You have no idea what to do or where to go next.

When you encounter any of the above feelings, it's likely a sign that you've reached the next magic turn on your writing path. Those feelings are little arrows pointing the way to an unknown direction. Remember: what we don't know is always going to be bigger than we imagine, and our creative curiosity keeps us on the edge of the unknown. Cultivate the courage to make invisible structures visible. Hang out with the uncomfortable questions and keep asking new ones.

The trick is to stay curious at this point and not play it safe by giving up. Instead, accept the discomfort so you can continue exploring unknown territory.

Not knowing but continuing anyway can feel impossible, but only if you believe that you're meant to feel in control of your writing. Remember, you're collaborating with a creative force. You don't want to be 100 percent in charge of your output. You can't be.

When you continue despite not-knowing, you'll start to create change, and your writing may teach you something new. You want to be surprised as a writer; that's how you know your reader will feel surprised, too.

When that zesty feeling starts to wane, I hope a little bell rings in your mind to signal your next-level inspiration: Here is where your story gets interesting. Here is where your writing is asking you to be even more curious.

Let your writing lead you. Be willing to let go of control and walk backwards. You may feel a little sick to your stomach. That's okay. Cry a little. Laugh maniacally. Lie on the floor and stare at the ceiling. Just for a minute or two. Then get back to your writing.

PRACTICE

Here are some practices to help you write through uncertainty:

- Engage in creative restriction: Set a timer, use a prompt, or set a deadline, a specific word or page count (like 376 words exactly).

- Copy the structure / form of another story or book you love.

- Play "What if?": Make a list of everything that could happen next, from boring to outlandish, and then pick one thing as a starting point and write it.

- Participate in a guided writing session facilitated by someone else.

- Write a hundred unconnected sentences from one point of view. Then read them out loud and see if there is a story there.

- Ask yourself a story-related question just before you go to sleep.

- Listen to a piece of music that reliably puts you in a trance; try binaural beats.

- Pair up with a writing friend: Commit to writing two to five pages a day, no matter how crappy they turn out to be.

- Practise deep noticing: Focus on one small detail in a scene and describe it at length, going micro or macro, without writing any action at all.

I encourage you to try one (or all!) of the above techniques to see if you can get more comfortable writing in a state of uncertainty. With practice, you'll recognize the potential within the weird feelings that accompany creative curiosity, and you'll recognize them for what they are: a sign that you've reached a turning point.

*

DEEP NOTICING

When I run my Story Is a State of Mind writing retreats in person, the goal is to develop a pattern of writing with presence and creative curiosity. I have a variety of practices I've shared with writers over the years, but this one is my favourite. I tried it for the first time with a group of writers in Italy.

Every day on our retreat, I asked my writers to start by writing down a list of ten things they had noticed that day so far. Then each writer would read one or two observations to the whole group.

One morning, a writer wrote, "The dark hole in the wall."

After she read this plain observation out loud, a palpable ripple passed through all of us. Because that dark hole, observed purely and documented without any mediation or explanation, suddenly existed in the air around us. We could feel it when she read it. It was real.

This simple yet profound observation brought the group's attention to the power of presence in writing. I call this deep noticing.

Deep noticing is about truly seeing what's in front of you, without your mind jumping in to label or explain it. This heightened state of awareness bypasses the tendency to immediately categorize or narrate what you see. It's a way to look at the world with fresh eyes. When you practise deep noticing, you're allowing yourself to experience the raw aliveness of each moment, each object, each scene.

This kind of seeing goes beyond just observing details—it's about connecting with the essence of what you're looking at. As a writer, when you tap into this way of perceiving, you're accessing a rich well of sensory information. You aren't thinking or analyzing; you're being present and receptive.

The magic of deep noticing is that it strips away the stories we habitually tell ourselves about what we see. Instead, it lets the world speak to us directly, in its own language of colours, textures, movements, and energies.

The moss on the edge of that piece of wood, for instance. It's profound as it is. A thread hanging off a boy's sock—it's important already. That slice of pear in your salad today? It has significance all on its own. You can make anything meaningful by giving it your attention. Just notice what it really is, feel the realness of it, and write that down. This seemingly simple act can be transformative for your writing.

By capturing this unfiltered presence on the page, you elevate everyday observations into unexpected insights. Your writing becomes a conduit for that heightened state of awareness, allowing readers to experience the world with fresh eyes, through your words.

This approach to writing transcends time, space, and context. It taps into universal human experiences and emotions. It acts as a bridge, connecting writer and reader in a shared space of awareness and connection. In essence, deep noticing invites your readers to see the world as you do in those moments of pure perception. It's a way of saying, "Look at this with me," and sharing the wonder of truly seeing.

When you notice the way sunlight plays on a bird's feathers, or how a person's hands move when that person speaks, the very act of acknowledging these details as they truly are imbues them with energy. In her poem "The Summer Day," Mary Oliver writes about observing a grasshopper eating cake at a friend's birthday party. Oliver describes what she sees with these lines:

the one who is eating sugar out of my hand,
who is moving her jaws back and forth instead of up and down—
who is gazing around with her enormous and complicated eyes.

As we read her words, we are seeing the same grasshopper. This shared experience transcends intellectual explanation. This is the power of deep noticing.

Noticing in general is an essential creative writing skill. It can be surprisingly difficult to restrict your active mind to notice something without making a story out of it right away. But you get much better details when you pause your impulse to narrate by default.

This practice isn't just a skill for writers; it's a way of experiencing the world that can enrich both your writing and your life. Make deep noticing a daily practice to cultivate this heightened awareness. You'll open yourself to the subtle textures of existence, allowing your unconscious mind to absorb and process these pure observations. Later, when you write, these unfiltered perceptions can arise as vivid, authentic details that bring your work to life. You get to use them however you want, because you're no longer limited by your usual expectations.

PRACTICE

This is a great warm-up and a stunning daily practice to try before you start working on your writing project.

Set a timer and then sit down with your bullet journal. Give yourself only ten minutes for this exercise but be sure to do it every day for one week.

Here it is: Write down a list of ten things you have noticed so far in your day.

Come into your body: Move your awareness away from interior thinking and into observing your environment. Focus on external details that involve your five senses. Be curious and patient. Let your observations come to you naturally. Don't explain what you notice or write what you think about each detail. Instead, allow your noticing to be the peak of your action. Stay present with minimalism. Avoid metaphors and overdescription.

If you write in the morning before you do anything else, don't worry. Even if it's 4:00 a.m., I promise you'll have already noticed ten things. Things like the colour of the light on your bedroom wall before the sun rises. The smell of coffee. The cool sensation of air passing through your nose as you breathe. The sound of a car outside your window. You get the idea. Be plain. Write simple, basic details.

Allow your observations to live on the page without meaning. Just jot down each little thing you notice, then write the next thing. Do this until you have ten observations or until your timer rings.

When you are finished, put your pen down, close your journal, and continue on with the rest of your day. Again, repeat this every morning for the next seven days.

You'll gradually notice patterns of awareness. This is not the same as patterns of thought. Deep noticing teaches you how to recognize your own way of seeing, to understand your non-verbal intelligence, and to learn, and better understand, your personal symbology.

This practice trains your ability to notice before thinking, as you are writing. The energy of your attention will inform the direction of your story—and it may not go where you think it should go. You can trust it. Follow that energy and practise putting your attention into words without knowing what it means right away.

Work with this energy in these daily lists so that it becomes inherent. When you're writing your next draft, this is a skill you'll need in order to put your vibrant, complex, multi-faceted story into words.

ABSTRACTION IS ARMOUR

When you find yourself writing about intellectual concepts rather than concrete details that a reader can physically feel, you've moved into abstraction.

Abstraction can be seductive because it lets writers use intellect and language in clever ways. It's also a way for you to feel in control, especially when you're writing emotional moments that require vulnerability.

Leaning into abstraction is like wearing armour as you write.

Abstraction labels a concept, and in so doing it protects you from feeling that concept. For example, *fear, happiness, frustration,* or *confidence* are all names for emotional sensations. Use abstract words like these sparingly in your creative writing. They lead your story into the realm of the mind and separate your reader from physical experience. Conversely, writing with sensory details brings embodied presence and a more immersive reading experience.

Feeling is transmitted in our writing through words, but the words themselves are not the feeling. Rather, they are the conduit through which the reader experiences the emotion. When you use concrete, sensory details instead of abstract labels, you allow the reader to inhabit a feeling instead of merely recognizing its name.

In the sentence "When they see each other, they feel the strength of their love and their kiss is full of passion," we understand what's happening conceptually, but we don't get to feel the passion, because the abstractions (*love* and *passion*) shield us from the sensations of intimacy. The words replace the feelings.

Imagine reading the same scene and feeling the softness of their lips as they touch, and the warm prickle of electricity over their skin as their heartbeats quicken. You don't have to use the words *love* or *passion* to understand what they're feeling.

Look for places where you're using abstract language in your writing and see if you can rewrite with more vivid details. When describing your characters' emotions, close your eyes and imagine yourself in the scene. What specific sensations do you notice? Look for concrete details that signal feelings: a clenched fist, a twitching eyebrow, or a waver in a voice. Notice your own body's responses as you imagine your characters' actions: What happens to your breath, your heart rate, your energy? These reactions will guide you toward more authentic descriptions. Using specific, sensory language to explore feelings on the page can give your writing a hum of immediacy.

PRACTICE

Write two short scenes that describe someone who is grocery shopping. Write the first scene from the point of view of someone who has just fallen in love. Write the second scene from the point of view of someone who has just lost their job.

In both instances, don't name the emotional state of the shopper. Don't use any abstract language to describe their feelings. Instead, simply write the details of the scene from each person's point of view.

In both scenes, the setting is the same: a grocery store. But when the person in love shops, she sees things differently and feels things differently than the person who is newly unemployed.

When you write concretely, paying attention to the sensory details in your scenes, you can infuse those details with the emotions you want your reader to feel. In this way, you let people experience your story using their own embodied presence.

*

THE READER BECOMES
THE CHARACTER

You've written a piece that feels tight, polished, and ready. You've revised it so many times that there aren't any typos or slips in point of view—it's clean. Your writing group loves it. You've been sending it out to short story contests and lit mags. But for some reason, it keeps getting rejected. What are you missing?

Well, maybe nothing. Stories get rejected way more than they get published, and not because they aren't good stories. If that's the case, you just have to keep going.

But it's also worth considering whether you're filtering too many of your scenes.

Filtering occurs when your scenes unnecessarily draw attention to your character's consciousness. This filter of consciousness can have a dulling effect on the immediacy of an otherwise vibrant scene.

For example: "I looked out the window and saw a blue car park in front of the house across the street."

That sentence has a filter on it. You're aware of the person seeing. It's subtle, but this is an extra cognitive step your reader has to make. When there are too many filters in your sentences, it may be hard for your reader to connect to your character.

This disconnection happens unconsciously—an editor might not even realize why she doesn't connect to your character. She just won't feel a zing.

Consider how the same moment in your story feels more alive when you write it this way: "A blue car parked in front of the house across the street."

In the unfiltered sentence, the car exists. You can see it. The character's presence is implied because you've established a point of view. The reader becomes the character seeing the car. There is no filter between the reader and the experience.

Written this way, your scenes can become consciousness.

If you write about your character seeing something, you remind your reader that she's reading about a character. You point to a character's consciousness—she has vision and is using it to navigate her world—and you miss the opportunity to give an unmediated experience to your reader.

Writing filtered consciousness asks your reader to peer into a diorama and imagine the story playing out inside the box. Writing unfiltered consciousness is letting your reader live the story as if she's inside the diorama.

Removing all of your filters might not work for every kind of prose or in every context. And, of course, using or not using filters depends on the effect you're going for in your writing. But in my experience, almost all scenes are sharper and more vivid when filters are removed.

As an experiment, start by cutting places where you label a character as "seeing" something in your story. Instead, write the details of what the character sees. If she sees a bird, describe the bird through her eyes. Just don't tell us she's seeing it.

Qualifiers like "I think," "We realize," "She sees," "He feels," and "They hear" are other little flags to look for as you review your story to remove unnecessary filtering.

For a deeper exploration of how to write vivid, unfiltered scenes, I recommend *From Where You Dream* by Robert Olen Butler, which provides the source of much of my insight on how filters affect writing.

*

MAKE ROOM FOR THE PASTRY CHEF

If you're feeling boxed in by your own productivity, if you feel you've reached a creative plateau, it might be time to more purposefully reactivate your creative curiosity.

Your imagination is driven by the creative centres of your brain. To stimulate them, give these parts of your brain more opportunities to do what they love to do.

Think of it this way: Your imagination is an amazing pastry chef. She can't wait to play in your kitchen. She would love to dazzle you with an assortment of beautiful and delicious treats, and she's waiting for an invitation.

How can you let her know that you value her talents and that you're eager to taste her recipes? Give her access to the pantry. Make room for her to show you what she can do in the kitchen.

Many writers have active minds that are attuned to problem-solving and pattern-making. When we add unresolved life stress, anxiety about world events, and a to-do list full of unreasonable deadlines, our minds can go into overdrive. It's hard to find time to let your imagination make flaky croissants when you're juggling so many worries and obligations, and it's tough to feel creative when you feel anxious.

Start your day by practising imaginative productivity. This kind of productivity requires you to change the gaze of your mind. You know those drawings where you can see one image in the drawing, but when you look at it another way, a second image emerges from the negative space? That's one example of the effect of changing your mind's gaze.

Imaginative productivity comes when you shift your mind into receptivity—noticing, looking, hearing, touching, and tasting. This is about setting yourself up to encounter things outside the conscious and unconscious boundaries your thinking mind has created.

Engage in deep noticing by allowing your curiosity to explore your surroundings (see page 97). Give yourself the time to truly see what's around you. With your bullet journal and pen, spend ten minutes listing things you hadn't noticed before. This focused practice, which you can integrate into your daily routine, serves as a brief yet powerful way to sharpen your awareness, an essential part of your creative warm-up.

There are other ways to reactivate your creative curiosity: look to another genre of writing or read other kinds of literary work, to remind you why you're writing and to teach you new ways to do it.

Take in other forms of art. Art disrupts patterns. It finds new and unusual connections, offers the gift of surprise, and short-circuits our habitual thought patterns. In other words, art gives our consciousness back to us.

Go to a concert. How do harmony and rhythm show up in your sentences?

See a play. Pay attention to the stage lighting. How would you write your scenes if you were a lighting director?

Look at sculpture. What can it show you about your book's structure, balance, density, and form?

Watch a dance performance. How does movement in the body create emotion?

Make a change in your physical surroundings or add a new physical sensation to your regular routine. The key here is to create a new experience for your body. Your mind and your body aren't separate. If you want to have a new mental experience, don't start by thinking—start by moving.

When your body encounters something new, it has to adapt to understand it. This adaptation creates a little biochemistry cocktail that can activate a new way of seeing. When you alter your normal way of doing things, your nervous system responds by sending signals throughout the body, and this can activate your imaginative mind.

Move your furniture around. Give your hands something to play with at your desk: a squishy ball, a helium-filled balloon, or juggling bags. Try a new form of movement: yoga, hula hoop, trapeze, forest running. Take an unusual route home from work.

This is creative exploration; it's inherently unpredictable. Something new will happen when you trigger your imagination. Let yourself be surprised.

As you purposefully use imagination more in your daily life, you'll begin to integrate these new modes of thinking and being into all kinds of practices. Notice what happens to your writing as a result.

*

RELEASE AN OLD
WRITING DECISION

I once said goodbye to an old raincoat. I'd had it for over fifteen years. I'd brought it with me on a writing retreat in Spain, teaching in Banff, and to the Victoria Festival of Authors. I have very pleasant memories associated with that coat.

It even used to keep me dry. It was so old, it stopped repelling water, but I kept wearing it. Why? Because it was *my* raincoat. It fit me, I knew it travelled well, it had a place in my closet. I don't know—my reasons weren't rational. Maybe I just remembered the way it used to keep me dry?

Eventually, I replaced it with a new one. And go figure: The new one is way better. It has more features! It's lightweight. The pockets are deeper. The lining is removable. The advanced waterproof fabric makes water bead off and roll away. Wow.

Had I known that I'd love my new raincoat so much, I would have replaced my old one long ago.

Beliefs work the same way as a raincoat: They protect us from the elements, reassure us with their practicality, and keep us comfy in a way that matches our personal style. But over time they can wear out or stop performing, and if we don't replace them, we may find ourselves feeling frustrated and uncomfortable.

Think of a limiting belief you have about yourself as a writer, or a limiting decision you've made about your work. It may have served you well at some point—otherwise, you probably wouldn't have kept it for so long.

And then think about whether it's still working for you. Maybe you've outgrown it. Or maybe it stopped functioning properly. Here are a few examples of the kinds of beliefs and decisions writers can outgrow:

I'm an emerging writer.

I only write fiction.

I'm working on a book.

I'm an academic writer.

Writing is hard for me.

I'm not a reader, but I love writing.

I'm not good at writing dialogue.

I don't have the skills to write a novel.

Sometimes our beliefs can motivate us and or make our writing life possible. But if we don't update them, they can also hold us back.

For instance, believing you are a novelist can help you write your first novel. It keeps you working toward your finished manuscript. But holding tightly to this belief can also hold you back if you want to write short stories or poetry or creative non-fiction.

What have you decided about your writing? What do you believe about your writing that might not be true anymore?

Can you trust that it will be okay for you to let outdated beliefs go?

Can you trust that when you release them, you're making space to eventually embrace a more empowering belief?

Without that old belief, who would you be?

If you let old beliefs go, what new things might you write?

*

STAY IN THE PROCESS

Do you feel like you don't know what you're doing? Do you fear that you're falling behind or working too slowly? That you can't tell if your writing is good or bad?

You're feeling all the normal feelings.

When I first sit down to write, I feel like I don't know what I'm doing either. I'm not being glib: I honestly feel like I'm starting from scratch every day. The thought crosses my mind as soon as I pick up my pen: *Can I do this? Really? How?*

I always find the clarity I seek through the process of writing itself. Writing is an act of discovery. As I write, insights emerge that weren't apparent to me before.

I remind myself of this all the time. I remember that I love writing because it stimulates my intuition, and that's also why I feel uncertain until I am in process. Once I remember this, I relax. I know that everything else will fall into place when I shift into a whole-minded state by allowing my creative mind and logical mind to work together. The mystery of writing requires my full attention and presence. Writing takes as long as it takes.

These are things that might leave you feeling like you're spinning your wheels rather than being productive: a general sense of frustration with your craft, demands from other parts of your life, or even daydreaming about sales and marketing. It can be seductive to dream about your final cover or your book tour, but ultimately these thoughts are keeping you from actively writing, let alone writing with creative curiosity.

When you're feeling uncertain about your writing, other tasks—whether it's finding the perfect new pair of yoga pants or cleaning the house—become more appealing because they're solvable in a way that mysterious, creative work is not. One way to avoid falling into a procrastination trap is to separate your writing time from your to-do list and problem-solving. Set clear boundaries for your writing time and honour them rigorously. If you haven't already established a writing schedule, create one now and treat it as sacred. During this time, focus solely on your writing, letting other tasks wait until your designated writing session is complete.

If you're struggling to stay in process, read. Read even more than you think is necessary. Read to understand craft and read for fun. This won't feel as productive as you think it should, and you won't have much to show for it for a while. But reading is one of the ways you can give yourself permission to delve into a different aspect of the writing process, a change of perspective that is focused on input rather than output. Reading widely exposes you to diverse styles, ideas, and narrative techniques, quietly informing and enriching your own writing. It's a form of passive learning that can spark creativity and help you overcome writing blocks.

If, at a cocktail party, someone asked about your work and you shared the titles of the books you were currently reading, they might think you hadn't heard their question correctly. What they don't know is that all the seemingly unproductive acts that happen around writing—reading, daydreaming, decluttering, taking long walks, closing your eyes to fully appreciate the smell of rain on asphalt—are actually subtle and crucial activities that make writing possible.

The mystery of the process is what makes the magic happen on the page, and once you acknowledge this, you can embrace it fully. Celebrate it by allowing yourself to trust this process, to revel in the uncertainty, and to find joy in the act of creation itself. Let this celebration of the unknown bring energy to your writing, prompt you to walk more interesting and unusual trails, and help you discover things about your story you never knew existed.

PRACTICE

Just as a compass guides us through unknown territory, we can use simple questions to orient ourselves in our writing journey when things get murky. Here's a practice that can serve as your daily guide, especially when you're working on a longer manuscript, like a novel.

1. Before you start work on your writing project, set a timer for five minutes of freewriting.

2. Begin by writing down an open-ended question in your notebook, something like: *What is this story about?* or *What's important to me about this story?*

3. Explore whatever comes up. You might write about elements of your plot, characters, themes, or emotions. Don't worry about having a definitive answer to the question. Writing it down will awaken the part of your mind that seeks meaning—that's the direction your inner compass is setting for your creative journey.

4. If you stall or run out of things to say, rewrite the question. This act of rewriting can reset your internal compass, restarting the process of open-ended thinking, wondering, and freewriting.

5. Think of this freewriting as window-shopping your mind. The goal isn't to find the perfect answer but to notice what asking the question brings up for you. Write until your timer stops you.

6. Then begin working on your manuscript. You might feel ready to tackle a story problem or to write a new scene. Or you might not—and that's okay. Trust that asking the question and making space for wonder has set something in motion, like a compass needle gently moving toward your personal true north.

7. Repeat this exercise every day until you finish your current draft. Here are some more open-ended prompts that can reset your compass:

   • I want to write about...

- What my main character wants the most and will never get is.

- What I really wish I could understand is...

8. As you write, remember that your goal isn't to answer the question definitively. The point of asking the question is that it helps you orient your story. Let the question be your compass and write your scenes toward the answer, even if that answer appears to move further away the closer you get, like the horizon.

This practice, like reading or taking long walks, might not feel immediately productive. However, these seemingly unproductive acts are crucial to the writing process. They're ways of staying present in your creative journey, even when the destination isn't clear.

It's natural to encounter foggy patches and feel disoriented by how much you don't know. Whenever confusion sets in, it's a sign you're in the process of change. Let these questions be your compass. Trust the change process and keep writing. Your story is out there, patiently waiting for you to discover it.

*

THE BEST WRITING ADVICE ALWAYS CONTAINS PARADOX

If you're wondering if it's the right time to make a big creative step that feels risky—like sending a query letter to an agent, submitting to a contest, taking a leave of absence from your day job to focus on writing your memoir or the novel you've been thinking about for years—I have two pieces of advice:

1. Start now, before you feel ready.

2. Pause. Start when you feel ready.

Both are the right thing to do, depending on the context.

I've published my writing before it felt perfectly finished, ready, one hundred percent cooked—because if I waited until it felt done, I would continue revising it forever. I've also drafted a novel and stored it in a box for years because I didn't know what the story wanted. The writing needed to rest, and I needed to live a bit more of my life before I fully understood the story.

Done is a moving target; it's impossible to pin down. We're human beings and we're always changing. What matters is your current state—and the current state of your story.

You might be ready to publish your writing and delight your readers with it. Or you might be mastering a new skill and need to give yourself more time, even if you're eager to move on to the next thing. Your task is to find out which is true for you right now.

Sometimes taking action feels expansive and exciting. Sometimes power needs more time to consolidate. Approaching decisions with open-hearted curiosity is one way to ensure you make the right choice at the right moment. *Ready* is a choice you get to make.

PRACTICE

Here are three questions to help you find clarity around which direction to take.

1. What feels the most like fun?

2. What feels the most life-giving?

3. Where is the current of energy?

As you ask these questions, pay attention to the responses from your mind and body. These are clues: answers may come to you in the form of words, images, or emotions. You may not get answers at all. That's okay. The work of this exercise happens in the asking.

＊

YOU'RE A WRITER

When Junot Díaz was asked whether winning the Pulitzer affected him, he answered, "As a writer? Not so much. In the end it's still just me and the blank page, me sitting down trying to figure out how to write this damn thing, you know?"

It's nice to remember that all the writers you love are doing their work the same way you are. After all, a writer is, at heart, someone who *writes*.

The next time someone asks you what you do, tell them you're a writer. Watch what happens to your breath when you say it out loud. How do the words sound? How does it feel? Does anything change in your body?

Two basic emotions are fear and love. Paying attention to your breath is a handy barometer: it can show you when you're feeling fear and when you're feeling love.

It took me many years before I called myself a writer with love. I thought I needed a permission slip before I could really earn the title—a certain kind of credential, a list of publications, some external validation that would check that box and provide proof. Eventually, though, I realized there is one single, solitary requirement to being a writer: that I write.

But knowing that and embodying it are two different things. When I first tried telling people I was a writer, my breath went shallow and my chest tightened up. I knew it was true as a concept, but I was afraid to say it out loud.

So I practised bringing love into the equation as an antidote to fear. Because the truth is, I *love* writing. Acknowledging that out loud feels right, and doing so gradually helped me open up to stating it clearly without losing my breath: I love writing. I love being a writer. *I am a writer.*

Once you know that you're a writer and you can embody the identity—and you can freely say so out loud—making time for your writing becomes much easier. It's non-negotiable. It's who you are.

*

FREEDOM, NOT FORCE

Many years ago, I was exhausting myself as I tried to write my second book. My first book took me ten years to write, and then, to my surprise, it was accepted by a publisher and selected for a prestigious literary prize. This experience changed the course of my professional life.

I worked really hard to write my first book, and I was extremely lucky to have it published. But in the years that followed that accomplishment, I was gripped by internal pressure: I felt that I was supposed to write another book that would match or surpass the literary success of my first book.

Or else.

Or else what? Honestly, I didn't even know. I was just terrified to fail. I tried to write work that people would judge as even more intelligent and more successful than my first book. But the truth was, I didn't like working so hard on my writing, contorting my words into forms that I hoped were literary, smart, and cool.

It was good for me to strive for excellence—until it wasn't anymore. Trying not to fail as a writer made me miserable.

I was telling myself that I had to write a certain kind of story to be a "real" writer, that I had to sound a certain way to be accepted by society, and that my writing career depended on me showing up in a way that made sense to other people. People I didn't even know! These were all lies that I was telling myself every day, and they made me feel more and more uncomfortable in my own skin.

When I began telling myself the truth, I did so quietly, at first, just in my journal. "I want writing to feel like freedom," I wrote. "I just want to write and be Sarah."

One day in our shared co-working space, I whispered my truth to a dear friend I'll call TJ. "I want to write a novel that is fun to read," I told her, looking over my shoulder to be sure nobody else was listening. "And... I want to have fun writing it."

TJ raised her eyebrows at me, as though I'd just admitted that I wanted to go skinny-dipping in a public pool. She understood the illicit nature of my confession. TJ herself was in MFA recovery, having left her program before undertaking her thesis defence. She'd gone rogue and was now writing phenomenally funny and smart personal essays. She was even publishing her writing herself, online, with no agent or publisher, like some feral creature raised by wolverines!

What I didn't know back then: my feelings of heaviness and fear were a signal from my true nature, distress flags that were trying to tell me something about what I did want to write. They were telling me the truth without words, using physical feelings and emotional waves.

I didn't know how to listen. I felt blocked, and I just kept pushing against my own energy, telling myself more stories about what I had to do to get over this creative hurdle. I found the solution, and it didn't come from forcing myself to push harder. It came from letting go.

I signed up for a six-week class with life coach Martha Beck called The Integrity Cleanse. In those six weeks I learned the importance of recognizing that a lot of the stuff I was telling myself about my writing wasn't true. Once I learned how to recognize a lie, I could steer myself in the opposite direction.

This changed everything. Up to that point I thought that the heavy, tight, compressed feeling I had was just how it felt to be a writer. It's not! When you're steering toward your truth, writing can feel like freedom.

Back to Martha Beck: in her book, *Finding Your Own North Star*, she introduces the concept of a Body Compass to help readers identify their truth. As a writer, I've adapted this into a practice for creative attunement. The goal is to show you when you're cultivating creative flow as opposed to forcing words onto the page. Here's my version for writers.

PRACTICE

1. Think about a time you forced yourself to write something that didn't feel right for you, your voice, your story, or your character.

2. Notice how your body reacts to the memory of writing through force. Describe any sensations in your body and what they look/smell/sound/feel like. (For me, force feels like my skin is heavy, thick, and tight. My throat feels compressed.)

3. Take a Post-it Note and at the top write *Force* as the title. Then jot down those descriptive words underneath.

4. Next, recall a time when your writing flowed effortlessly, and the words felt true to your project.

5. Notice how your body reacts to this memory of writing with freedom. Describe where in your body you feel any sensations and what they look/smell/sound/feel like. (For me, flow feels cool, my chest is light and free, my throat is open, and I have a sparkly feeling at the top of my head.)

6. On a second Post-it Note, write *Freedom* at the top as the title. Then write down those descriptive words underneath.

7. Put these two Post-it Notes where you can see them as you write, as a reminder.

Now you have a personal compass you can use to help you write your next essay, book, or scene! Use these feelings to turn toward what is right for you and your writing. Even if you don't understand why a dress must be purple, or why it also needs to have green ribbons on it, your body will probably tell you—whenever you try to write it a more "reasonable" colour, like yellow, you're likely to feel one of the feelings on your *Force* list.

It's like playing warmer/colder with your work in progress. You can trust your body.

Eventually, you won't need the Post-it Notes anymore. You'll know how to follow freedom by heart and write what your story wants you to write, not what you're telling yourself you *should* write.

When you're writing from that place of freedom—where you feel alive, curious, and focused, or any of the other words that appear on your *Freedom* list—you'll experience deep enjoyment, a hallmark of the flow state.

Writing my second book wasn't always easy, but I did have a lot of fun writing it. I approached it with fresh eyes and wrote every scene with those two Post-it Notes stuck to my desk as reminders of how I did, and didn't, want to feel. And when I felt that familiar lightness in my chest and the sparkles at the top of my head, I knew I was on the right track.

*

VISUALIZE THE FINISH

Let your unconscious mind help you move your story toward completion.

I first learned this approach from Al Watt's *The 90-Day Novel*, and it has profoundly shaped my writing process.

Your unconscious mind pays attention to landmarks like colours, emotions, and sensations. It has a natural tracking instinct—the ability to see patterns and notice connections without your conscious awareness. To harness this instinct and get it to lead you to the end of your story, you have to give it signs and images it can understand. This is like giving a tracking dog an object with a person's scent and then setting the dog loose in a forest; she'll bring you to your destination by following her nose.

In your case, tracking will happen in your unconscious mind as you read, as you listen to conversations around the dinner table, as you travel, shop, work, watch TV—even while you're sleeping. You don't have to know how you'll get to the ending. You don't have to know every scene you're going to write on the way there. You just need to set the coordinates of your inner GPS and establish landmarks to guide the way to your final destination.

Set up key landmarks by imagining your character at the end of their story. Decide on your desired word count or number of pages, and then enjoy the journey. The path to your story's conclusion will naturally emerge through your writing.

I wrote my novel, *Radiant Shimmering Light*, using Al Watt's book as a guide. In my visualization of the final scene, I saw my protagonist at the edge of a pond, gazing into the water, watching minnows swimming. I did not know the significance of this detail. The book had nothing to do with fish! I was baffled, but I kept going, writing one thousand words a day as he suggested. When I reached the final pages of my first draft, I found my protagonist gazing out at the ocean and seeing a whale. I felt a full-body shiver and set down my pen. I knew I'd reached the end.

PRACTICE

In Part 1 of the practice below, I elaborate on Al Watt's technique of visualizing the end of a story, and I include my own reflection prompts. Part 2 adds an additional practice of visualizing yourself as the writer who finishes writing the book.

These practices are versatile and great to use in different phases of your writing project—at the very beginning, during planning and outlining, whenever you feel stuck, during revisions, and when you're near completion. They help keep you motivated, aligned, and consistent.

Part 1: Your character at the finish

1. In your mind's eye, visualize your character at the end of the story. Imagine a point where all of the subplots and story elements are resolved, harmonized, settled. You don't need to know how it all happens: just skip to the very last scene. How does your character feel at this moment? What images come into your mind? Describe the setting: Where are they? Who are they with, if anyone? What has changed in your character's physiology, environment, or mental/emotional state? Use all five senses to experience this scene. These details are clues from your unconscious mind and will become your landmarks.

2. Freewrite in your notebook about the images and information you received in step one. You might find yourself writing full scenes (e.g., your character laughing, or sleeping, or saying key pieces of dialogue out loud) or describing symbols for which you don't have the full context (e.g., a boat anchor, a robin's egg, or a pair of cowboy boots). Don't overthink it. First thoughts are best thoughts here, and because they're coming from your creative unconscious, it's okay if the images don't make sense to you yet. These are your landmarks.

3. Set these landmarks aside, and come back to your writing practice. Stay flexible and focused by centring yourself before each writing session: you want to be present and oriented towards the ending, even if you're still at the beginning of the writing journey.

    Use one or two of the following prompts for about ten minutes of freewriting; do this as often as you like. This will help you check in and spark the tracking instinct that runs behind the scenes in your mind, while also reinforcing your landmarks.

I will know I'm at the end of my story when...

My story's completion feels like...

When the conflict is harmonized, it looks like...

My story will know it's finished when...

I know I've reached the outcome when I write this...

Part 2: You at the finish

For this visualization, you are going to imagine yourself actually writing the final scene of your book. This is especially useful if you're prone to believing that finishing a book is difficult or impossible. Use this exercise to replace that old belief with this new one by creating personal landmarks that show the reality of completion.

1. Picture yourself writing the final scene of your book. How does your future self feel at this moment? What images come to mind? Describe the setting: Where are you? Who are you with, if anyone? What has changed in your physiology, environment, or mental/emotional state? Use all five senses to experience this scene.

2. Write these details down in your bullet journal. As you freewrite this scene about yourself in the future, keep

layering in more details. Think about the colours and textures you'll be experiencing in that moment. Let yourself really see what it looks like, hear what it sounds like, and feel what it feels like. Keep adding details until the scene feels real. These details become personal landmarks for you. The more you can see, hear, and feel in this imagined moment, the stronger your connection to your goal becomes. Use your imagination to capture vivid and specific details from your vision of the future. For example, *When I finish writing this book, it's January 7th. There's a candle burning on my desk, filling the room with the scent of sandalwood. I'm wearing a green wool sweater. The branches of the cedar tree outside my window are covered in snow. When I type my last word, I smile, and then I stand up and stretch my arms over my head. I feel clear and calm.*

3. Notice the way finishing your book feels different than working on your book. Where do you feel the sensation of completion in your body? Pay attention to the physiological sensations that indicate you're "done." These feelings might be literal (e.g., warmth in your chest or a shiver down your spine), or metaphoric and symbolic (e.g., "done" feels like deep blue light filling your chest or the perfect symmetry of a smooth, round stone sitting on your desk). Write these down in your bullet journal, too. These sensations are internal landmarks that signal completion.

4. Ground yourself in this visualization by regularly revisiting it before you begin writing. Use one or two of the following prompts for about ten minutes of freewriting; do this as often as you like. This will train your unconscious mind to bring you to your destination without your conscious mind being aware of it.

I will know I'm at the end of my story when I…

When my project is complete, I will feel…

I will know I have finished when I see / hear…

I will know my story is complete when I no longer…

When my project is finished, I will have learned…

Working in alignment with your unconscious mind can make finishing a project much easier; it's like having the wind at your back. Once you've set the scene and given your unconscious mind these various landmarks—from story details to personal visualizations to your physical sensations—you don't have to do anything other than show up as planned and keep writing. The route to your destination will be revealed through your writing practice. Your unconscious mind will guide you there.

＊

WRITE UNDER THE INFLUENCE

We uncover new depths in our writing when we notice what other writers have done, when we connect to their work, and when we respond to it with our own.

The time you spend as an active reader is as important as the time you spend writing at your desk. Read widely. "Write what you know" doesn't mean writing only about your family, your memories, your experiences. It means writing with everything you've encountered in your own life and through other experiences—including reading.

The truth is, you're going to be influenced by everything you read—forever. This is a good thing! Embrace it.

Read authors who inspire you. Read books that puzzle you. Read lots of different genres, lots of different writers, and read about all kinds of subjects. Read to learn about style, language, structure, and character development. Read for entertainment. You absorb knowledge through your experience of reading—the more widely you read, the more possibilities you'll see for your own writing.

Your unique writing voice and style isn't a fixed or perpetual form. It doesn't appear all at once on the page. It's developed over time, and it is sculpted by your environment.

Make a choice to be influenced, and use reading to your advantage. What would your story be like if you wrote your sentences like Sheila Heti? How would your scene change if you used dialogue like Thomas King? If you were Ruth Ozeki, how would you organize your novel's timeline?

As with all new experiences, you learn more when you consciously pay attention to what you're doing. There's no need to be afraid that you might start to sound like other authors: this is a legitimate part of your development as a writer. Learning a skill by studying with a master is apprenticeship. Before we understand how to create our own delicious meals, we follow recipes. The more you purposefully read for influence, the more textured your own voice will become. Your writing will get stronger and more interesting as you learn new styles.

A caveat: There's a difference between plagiarism and influence. Influence is doing something in the same style or manner as someone else. Plagiarism is copying the same words or including identical elements of a story, especially without credit. Influence asks for our humility, and plagiarism works with our arrogance. Allowing yourself to be influenced is a sign of respect, but copying someone else is a sign of fear and insecurity. Check in; you can feel the difference.

I learned how to use influence in my own writing from my mentor and thesis advisor, the brilliant author Zsuzsi Gartner. She challenged me to read and write short stories that pushed me way out of my comfort zone, and to exceed my own perceived limits by purposefully imitating George Saunders's short story "The Falls." His story uses a third-person omniscient point of view that shifts between multiple characters, and the sentences are intricate and often darkly humorous. Trying to match his sentence structure and cadence challenged me to write in a completely different way. The experience taught me that I could do much more with language than I thought was possible. It also felt really weird and wrong at first.

You know when you try a new yoga stretch and it doesn't feel right because you're putting your body in an unfamiliar position? That's how you strengthen muscles and make your body flexible. It's the same when you try out new ways to write a story.

Writing under the influence might not feel good at first because it asks you to squeeze and stretch your sentences into shapes and lengths that are new to you. Give yourself time to write through the discomfort. This is how your writing voice evolves; with practice, new shapes can feel more comfortable. And if they don't, you can let them go. This is how you find and develop your style.

Have fun with influence. Write like someone else and try to enjoy how exhilarating it can be to push your boundaries. This is like going to a costume ball or fancy dress party—it's exploring by playing dress-up. Letting go of your own viewpoints and trying to write from new perspectives can multiply your creative options.

Keep an influence journal

Our writing shows us where we've been, where we are now, and where we want to go next.

When we let creative curiosity lead our writing practice, it might show us rugged mountain trails, smooth downhill slopes, flooding riverbanks, dark caves, infinite vistas, wildflower meadows, massive ocean waves, or mysterious tidal pools. Navigating these diverse elements enriches our work and makes us better writers.

It feels great when you find your groove and finally start writing with speed and momentum. It can also be satisfying to get out of your groove and face a challenge that stretches your abilities and reveals new dimensions of your craft's potential.

We move back and forth between polarities throughout our writing life. Explore, change, integrate, repeat. Getting familiar with these cycles can help you become a better writer and may lead to a writing life you truly enjoy.

In *The Art of Is: Improvising as a Way of Life*, Stephen Nachmanovitch shares his Notice, Connect, Respond theory and how it applies to improvisation and creativity. This framework encourages deep engagement with the world around us, and for writers, it can apply beautifully to the experience of reading.

One of the best ways to anchor this process is by focusing on, connecting with, and responding to what you're reading. Do this on purpose. Keep track of what you learn and give yourself inspired lessons and writing assignments for your future work.

Here are some actual notes from my own influence journal:

Peyakow by Darrel McLeod: Mix up visions of the future with dreams and memories. Let languages be as they are, and don't overtranslate.

Malibu Rising by Taylor Jenkins-Reid: Countdown to the last scene propels the narrative. Don't be afraid to add lots of characters and subplots.

Double Blind by Edward St. Aubyn: In a circular structure, the ending is ambiguous, and yet every character arc is resolved. End each of your chapters with a resonant sentence that could also end the whole novel.

No One Is Talking About This by Patricia Lockwood: Remember to float, dance, and play with the language. Let go of trying too hard to make sense. "Novel" can mean anything you want.

Writing down your reflections is also a great way to capture your personal themes and obsessions. It's fun to look back at your past entries to reflect on how you've grown as a writer. You'll notice how your creative focus changes over time, while some aspects remain constant. This process can reveal how your explorations both expand your horizons and reinforce your core identity as a writer.

The creative process is non-linear. Sometimes you go down a specific rabbit hole without knowing why, only to see details from that tangent emerge in your writing later, when you least expect it. Or a particular element of a story that interested you in the past becomes the surprise answer to your current writing problem.

Your influence journal is a valuable resource: it's a grimoire, a map, an instruction manual, a recipe book, and a field guide that you can consult throughout your writing life.

PRACTICE

Use your bullet journal as your influence journal. This practice will take advantage of the numbered pages and index at the front.

To prepare, reserve thirty pages in your bullet journal for this practice. In the index, note the page range you've reserved and title it *Influence Journal*. When you need more space, you can reserve another batch of blank pages later in your bullet journal and note this second batch in the index to keep it organized.

Part 1: Notice

1. On the first page reserved for your influence journal, make a list of five to ten books you've read recently (all genres, including cookbooks, self-help, poetry, thrillers, and romance, etc.).

2. Add five books that you loved as a child.

3. Now add five books you consider timeless classics—the ones you keep by your bed, gift to people you love, or keep as talismans on your shelf.

Part 2: Connect

1. Pick one title from each of your four lists.

2. On a new influence journal page, make notes about how each book has influenced you or how you'd like it to influence you. Ask yourself what you wish to absorb from each of these four titles. Use one of the following three prompts to get started:

    •   My writing loves this book because...

    •   This book wants me to know that I can...

    •   This book showed me how I could...

    You can also just jot down your own notes or follow your own prompts. The point is to put into words the learning that you've internalized.

Part 3: Respond

1. Review your notes and choose one lesson you've learned or are currently learning from one of those books—something that excites you or opens up a sense of possibility.

2. On your influence journal pages, write this lesson as a directive or assignment for yourself. For instance: "Try writing in second person point of view" or "Describe monsters with texture and smell instead of shape and size" or "Make your chapters super-short, like only one page each." Choose something concrete that you'd like to experiment with in your own writing. To stay orga-

nized, note the page number for this lesson in your bullet journal's index.

3. Now, pull out your freewriting notebook. Try your own assignment: depending on what your directive is, you might take ten minutes to do an experimental freewrite, or sketch out a possible structure, or write about something thematic.

Remember, an influence journal isn't meant to be a challenge, like reading a hundred books in a year or some other productivity game. It's more like a dream journal centred on your reading and writing practices.

You might not feel compelled to go back and revisit your journal entries. That's totally fine—you don't need to reread your notes for this to work. The learning happens as you actively notice, connect, and respond.

Keeping an influence journal can set your creative change in motion. As you put your insights into words, you're already making internal changes. You're allowing the influence to take root as you write about it.

By engaging deeply with what you read and reflecting on how it shapes your writing, you open yourself up to new possibilities and continuous growth as a writer. This practice can help you navigate your ever-changing creative journey, always moving forward while staying true to your own voice.

＊

TO BE A BETTER
WRITER, READ

Have you ever found yourself thinking something like, *If only N. K. Jemisin would read the first draft of my manuscript and give me feedback, I would be a better writer.*

If you can find one, a living, in-person mentor who gives you one-on-one attention is a wonderful writing support. Having a writer pay close attention to you and your work feels amazing. You might learn a lot from N. K. Jemisin's revision notes. But mentorship opportunities are rare because authors need so much time and space to devote to their own craft. Fortunately, mentorship isn't the only way to learn how to be a good writer.

So much of your growth as a writer depends on you paying close attention to what you're reading. In other words, if you really want to learn what N. K. Jemisin would think of your manuscript, read N. K. Jemisin.

Reading can be like dropping a stone in a body of water.

There's a splash, and then the water moves outward in a distinct pattern. To learn from what you read, you need to pay attention to the shape and structure of the ripples that form as a result of the splash.

Find an author you admire and read their work. Read their earlier books and see how the style compares to their more recent books. Read their work to study the patterns and variables that affect their writing. Do your research: read about how this person writes. Read their interviews. Read their novels, essays, articles, editorials, and writing contest introductions. Copy by hand passages of their work into your own notebook, to see if there is anything to be learned by stepping into their syntax and language. Read their book recommendations. Read their influences.

How you react to what you read teaches you who you are as a writer. Follow the clues of your own admiration and awe; even shadow emotions like sadness, jealousy, and repulsion can be teachers. Pay attention to what you notice. Write down what you feel and write down what you don't feel—by taking the time to put your feelings and responses into language, you make space to investigate the underlying messages and directions they might offer you.

Your *curiosity* teaches you about what you want to do next.

Your *affinity* teaches you about your values and true nature.

Your *admiration* teaches you about your own skills and abilities.

Your *sadness* teaches you what you love and find most meaningful in storytelling.

Your *jealousy* teaches you what you really want to do or have in your own work.

Your *repulsion* teaches you about your shadow and qualities you need to develop.

If you don't have an in-person writing mentor yet, don't let that get in the way of your study and practice. Don't wait for a mentor to come into your life before you begin your apprenticeship. The potential for learning lives on your bookshelves.

Books are your mentors, and to access their teachings, you only have to pay attention to what comes up for you as you read.

PRACTICE

1. Bring to mind a book you love. Maybe it's the book that helped you decide to start writing. Or the book you're comparing to yours, as you write your query letter. The book that's one of your secret influences. The book you're responding to in your current project—in your own voice and style. Choose a book that reliably motivates you or lights you up.

2. Ask yourself why you love it. What do you really appreciate about this book? How has it affected your writing? What have you learned from it? What do you love about it? Why do you connect to it so much? Freewrite your answers in your notebook.

3. Reflect on your appreciation. Notice whether the aspects you admire in the author's work are somehow present in

your own work. They may still be undeveloped, unseen, or in shadow, but you wouldn't recognize those qualities if you weren't already attuned to them. You might be exploring the same concepts within a different context. Your writing might have a similar cadence, pace, or style. Or one strikingly different from your previous work—their book might have inspired you to take a bold new direction. Write down whatever aspects of their writing you admire, and note any ways they might connect to your own work, either present or past.

4. Imagine the creative energy that powers the book you admire. Close your eyes and try to visualize it with your mind's eye. Give this energy a shape, a colour, a texture, a sound.

5. Now, imagine the creative energy that powers your own writing project. Keep your eyes closed and try to picture it in your mind. Again, visualize the shapes, colours, textures, and sounds of this energy.

6. Observe the ways in which these two creative energies are in alignment. Compare and contrast your visualizations, perceiving the similarities and differences in the shapes, colours, textures, and sounds. Watch as the creative energies overlap. Note how your own creative energy is part of a greater sphere of creative energy.

7. Write down your reflections. If you received any specific direction or insight from this visualization, write down what you learned.

*

BE A TWO-YEAR-OLD

Several summers ago, my friend came to visit with her two-year-old, Josephine. I was a bit nervous before they arrived: I don't spend a lot of time with children, and our home is not exactly childproofed. We keep our Cuisinart blades in a bottom drawer in the kitchen, for instance.

When Josephine entered the house, I held my breath. She gave me a wily look, as if to say, "Well, at least I'm finally out of that car seat. You better make this worth it!"

I showed her around our home. We decorate minimally, with mostly whites, neutrals, and wood. We don't have kids' toys or any of the colourful foamy stuff you see in the children's wing of IKEA. I let her lead me up the wooden staircase and into the library, feeling woefully unprepared for my tiny visitor. She was noticeably silent. Was our space any fun at all, as far as she could tell?

She looked up at my bookshelves. She sized up my laptop on the desk. I waited for her next move. I noticed her noticing.

Josephine was an excellent noticer. She noticed the piece of rainbow electrical tape I had wrapped around my old computer power cord. The glitter that stuck to her fingers after she touched a homemade bookmark. The weird sound of a baby blue jay out the window. The small sand-filled strawberry attached to my red pincushion.

She noticed these things. Like, she noticed them with her whole body.

Creative curiosity recognizes itself. Noticing her noticing, I felt awareness arise inside my body.

I had overscheduled myself that summer. My calendar was filled with a variety of back-to-back appointments, calls, and events. Spending time with Josephine that weekend was a wake-up call. I watched her move through her world with genuine openness: she was interested, playful, and curious. Her presence made my own curiosity flutter and spark, and reminded me that I needed to spend more quality time with my own true nature. That weekend, Josephine was my teacher.

The following Monday, I cancelled a third of my social events and work-related meetings scheduled for that week. And I mean cancelled: I didn't postpone or reschedule them. I felt radical and disobedient. I felt afraid, too—what would people think?

As it turns out, making time for noticing made *everything* in my life better.

I did not write that week. But I did increase my capacity for creative curiosity. And in just a couple of weeks, I surprised myself by writing an essay about Yayoi Kusama that was later published in an Australian literary magazine. The intentional pause gave me the chance to notice my fascination with Kusama's life and work, and I gathered my own insights effortlessly because I had given myself the space to do so.

This is a truth I've learned and relearned so many times in my life: For me, doing nothing always turns into deep noticing. The key is to simply continue to do nothing for long enough.

To be a good noticer, you have to let yourself get quiet enough to be present to what's actually happening. Back when we were two-year-olds and could only speak in two-word phrases, this happened more naturally for us. That part of our inner nature is still alive inside us, though, and it's always calling us to explore.

When I slow down on purpose, I go through a few days of weird nothingness before the antsy feeling slows down and shifts into noticing. Then, I begin to really see, hear, feel, smell, and taste again.

The initial discomfort that comes with clearing my schedule is worth it, because it turns into the joy of paying attention. After a few days of nothingness, once I adjust to the new pace of my life, I feel more than ready to write.

It's hard to pay attention when you have too many things to do. It's easy to notice things when you're not doing anything else. The dance between those two polarities of attention is a lifelong practice for writers.

Here's how you can make the first step in that dance.

PRACTICE

1. Cancel something today. Skip the meeting, the coffee date, the graduation party, whatever it is you had planned. You might feel flaky, unreliable, or rude. You might also feel afraid to cause disappointment or afraid of the consequences. That's okay. Making space is a radical act. You don't have to feel fearless before you take courageous action. (In fact, it's feeling afraid and doing it anyway that makes it courageous.)

2. Spend your new-found free time in white space. Do nothing. Don't declutter or clean up. Don't write or meditate. Just do nothing. Be a two-year-old. See what happens— and what you notice.

*

SOLITUDE AND INTERDEPENDENCE

Sometimes I really love to rattle around in my writing room all alone, like a witch-artiste with unbrushed hair, scribbling mysterious questions in notebooks, arranging my significant talismans—stones from the beach, glass beads, silk flowers, glitter stars, cut-out pictures of tigers, a blind contour drawing of a woman's face, a Japanese iron bell—on my windowsill altar.

When I get into this state, I don't feel unstable, though I know I might look it. I feel calm and energized—half the little kid I used to be and half imaginary grandmother from a fairy tale.

It's good for a writer to have a safe space in which to explore their creative state of mind without being seen or observed. Solitude can be a container for potent emptiness, possibility, and comfort. I am grateful to have a whole studio of my own for this kind of work, but any room with a door will do.

Creative curiosity unfastens you from the rigidity and ignorance of adulthood. It invites you to play deeply, the way you did when you were young. It opens you up to your intuition and to undiscovered wisdom you might have inherited from all sorts of places and never realized was within you.

This is an enchanted mix of energies. It's also a private one: very few people have actually witnessed me in this state. Magic happens when you can spend uninterrupted time with yourself. You might have your own version—a persona or style that comes alive when you have time to think and create by yourself.

I love to be alone with my thoughts. I love to watch movies by myself. I love to be alone on a hike in the woods. I love solo travel: driving down country roads, looking out the window on a train. I love to be alone in the library using headphones to listen to music that inspires me. But in an extrovert-dominant culture that is afraid of loneliness, solitude can sometimes seem suspicious. If you have internalized that point of view, you might have a habit of overlooking your own desire for alone time, which can become a pattern of neglecting your own needs.

Be kind to the part of yourself that thrives on aloneness and start to give it more of what it needs. To flourish, your creative curiosity might just need a little more solitude.

My husband, Ryan, understands this about me. After we moved in together, he learned that I wasn't kidding about how much alone time I needed. He even agreed to include it in our wedding vows. He protects my solitude, just like Rilke advised in *Letters to a Young Poet*.

However, while solitude is crucial for creative work, it's important to recognize that there can be too much of a good thing. There's a shadow side that can arise with too much solitude: the feeling of *I don't belong*.

Because our writing trains us to observe and take notes, writers often live and write on the fringes of society. When a healthy amount of solitude extends past a point of balance, writers can become anti-social, neurotic, and even seriously depressed or anxious.

Pay attention to your own balance. Remember that the point of your solitude is not to disconnect entirely from those you love or community but to discover magical insights you can bring back to others in the form of your writing. Design your retreats into solitude to give you the power to create more connection.

This delicate balance between solitude and connection brings us to an important concept: the interdependent writer.

As writers, we value our self-sufficiency. We value our solitude. Writing a book takes an extraordinary amount of self-direction. Self-discipline is one of our admirable qualities. But when we overvalue our independence, we run the risk of trying to solve all our problems by ourselves. This makes a writing life harder than it has to be.

Several years ago, I worked with a smart, talented writer named Ky, who came to my class with the goal of completing his novel. He prided himself on his self-reliance. When faced with a challenging plot hole in his manuscript, Ky spent weeks agonizing over it alone, refusing to bring his draft to class or to discuss the story elements with us. His progress stalled, and his frustration mounted. As far as I know, Ky is still working on his first draft in solitude, all these years later. This is a clear instance of how excessive independence can hinder a writer's growth and productivity.

Some independent writers even feel like their work is more valid when it's difficult—like Ernest Hemingway, who famously said, "There is nothing to writing. All you do is sit down at a typewriter and bleed."

While independence can be problematic, swinging to the other extreme isn't the answer either. Writers can also create a codependent dynamic with their work.

Writing is an essential, grounding activity for many writers. We feel the need to write. It helps us think, process our feelings, and confront our fears. It's therapeutic and fulfilling work. But when we tie our self-worth and emotional stability too tightly to our productivity, we can become trapped, with our sense of self and well-being rocked by the fluctuating waves of our creative process.

Take Maria, a poet and lyric essayist I know who found herself unable to face the day without writing at least one poem. On days when inspiration didn't strike, she felt worthless and anxious. Her mood swings were directly tied to her writing output, creating an unhealthy cycle of dependence on her craft. This illustrates how codependence in writing can negatively impact a writer's mental health and overall well-being.

Some codependent writers only feel truly alive when they're writing. Sylvia Plath is an example of this. As she said, "I write because the world is not enough, and words are the only way I can bridge the gap between reality and imagination."

Both Hemingway's and Plath's mindsets pathologize the act of writing and suggest that suffering is an inherent part of the creative process, which can exacerbate harmful mental tendencies a writer may already possess. It's crucial for every artist to understand that creative expression should not come at the cost of mental health.

It's true that writing can be both challenging and therapeutic. But when/if it becomes enmeshed with your sense of self-worth and emotional stability, it can lead to a dangerous cycle. If you find yourself experiencing distressing thoughts or feelings, please take good care of yourself and seek help. Your art does not require suffering. Your well-being matters just as much as your creativity and creative output.

There are potential pitfalls to both independence and codependence in writing. Fortunately, there's another approach.

As writers, we know how to use our imagination to create new narratives. So let's start telling ourselves a different story about what it means to be a writer. Can we let go of the old stereotypes and see writing as a way to express our love of life. Could we see it as a source of joy?

As your relationship to writing evolves, you get to make choices that feel more integrating than isolating. Instead of independence or codependence, choose to grow creatively in interdependence.

An interdependent writer is more likely to have a balanced and healthy relationship with writing and isn't afraid to ask for support. You value your writing but don't let it subsume your identity. Because you don't rely on writing to determine your sense of self-worth, you can more readily discover new ways to satisfy all the different but equally important parts of yourself. You feel grounded and awake to what interests you. You notice synchronicities. You genuinely respect, admire, and celebrate other writers' successes.

I like to think about my mentee Rosa, a successful novelist who embodies the principles of interdependence in her writing life. Rosa has a regular writing routine, but she's flexible when life throws her curveballs. She's part of a supportive writing group where she both gives and receives feedback. When stuck on a particularly challenging part of her work, she doesn't hesitate to reach out to me or another mentor for help. Yet, she also knows when to step back and let her work breathe. Rosa finds joy in other activities—watercolour painting, running, spending time with her family—which often inspire her writing in unexpected ways. Her success doesn't define her, nor does she feel threatened by other writers' achievements. Instead, she sees the literary community as a collaborative space where everyone's success contributes to the richness of the field.

Change your story about being a writer and you will change your experience of being. Orient your writing toward enjoyment instead of suffering.

See if you can recognize any of these signs that your relationship with writing might be out of balance:

You feel worried about sounding stupid or being incompetent, even when writing a first draft or exploratory scenes.

You struggle to solve craft and story problems until your brain hurts, you feel deeply fatigued, or even become ill.

Winning a contest or receiving a grant for your work feels good for a second, and then you feel anxious and inadequate.

You overthink your world-building until your structure becomes so complex that you resist writing the story itself.

You feel deeply jealous or threatened when you hear about another writer's success.

You emotionally disconnect and numb out in order to get a certain number of pages written each day, no matter what, but when you think about revising them, you feel a weight in the pit of your stomach.

You feel anxious, depressed, ungrounded, or distressed when you're not actively writing.

You constantly share your writing with others because you struggle to write when you aren't receiving feedback.

Receiving a rejection letter or negative feedback on your work can trigger an extended period of sadness, shame, or resentment, and you might even stop writing for a while as a result.

You have a hard time finishing your work because you're afraid you won't meet your own or external expectations.

You feel guilty when you take time away from writing to focus on other priorities, on your family, or on leisure.

If any of these feel familiar, I get it. I've been there. Let's explore the characteristics of a healthier, interdependent approach:

You know how to ask for and receive support from a writing coach, a friend, or a writing group. When you're stuck, you regularly reach out for help.

When your work is published or places in contests, you celebrate your accomplishment without letting it define you.

You know how to use discernment when it comes to feedback. There are times when you want to share your work for critique and times when you prefer to work on it privately. You value your own inner compass *and* you value the opinions of others.

You enjoy taking occasional breaks from writing and fully immerse yourself in other experiences—like relationships, travel, and hobbies—without guilt.

When a writing friend secures a fabulous agent or publishing deal, you're excited for them. You wholly celebrate the success of your peers—it feels like their wins are your wins.

I have great news: if you want to live a more balanced writing life, you can start right now.

PRACTICE

Here are two practices that will help you cultivate a more balanced, interdependent approach to your writing life. Try either one whenever you're feeling too independent or too codependent with your writing to bring things back into balance.

1. Track the moments of joy, synchronicity, pleasure, and abundance in your life. Use your bullet journal, or you

can use a separate notebook to specifically record these positive experiences. Write down these moments as they occur and review your list each morning and / or evening. Keep this notebook handy so you can look through it often, especially when you need a boost of positivity.

2. Consider ways you can create and honour positive writing friendships. Could you start a writing group or find a writing partner? Write a postcard to a poet friend once a week? Organize and host monthly co-writing calls? Sign up for a writing workshop? Take one step toward building your support network, so you have more places you can reach out to for help the next time you feel stuck.

Practising interdependence will help you maintain a healthy relationship with your craft.

*

WRITE THE FORBIDDEN

When a writer dares to write about tough subjects, they can disrupt the shape of the atmosphere. The smooth-as-fondant force field around what can't be expressed warps and disintegrates, and a reader can experience insights that come from bearing witness to forbidden knowledge, guilty pleasures, or secret activities.

Writing the forbidden stretches the boundaries of our capacity to understand the complex nature of being human. Like a mollusc that grows by adding new material to its spiralling shell, writers also continually add new layers of awareness to the narratives that become our shared cultural memories.

To boldly write what cannot be said or seen, you need some serious moxie.

Maybe you know how difficult it is to write the forbidden because you've tried it. There are topics and people you can't write about—even if you really want to—because you can't seem to find the words. Or you might have the right words but you're afraid to put them down—because someone might read them.

But the call to write about a forbidden subject is sometimes insistent, a whisper in the back of your mind that you can't quiet.

Your body might react; you may literally squirm in your seat, feel dizzy or nauseous, or break out in a cold sweat. The voices in your head warn you—*Do not go there*. It's like you've come across a strip of yellow caution tape designed to block you from entering a crime scene.

Here's the thing: you're the writer. That gives you official permission to lift the tape and enter the scene. Feel the electricity of your fear in your body, use your pen as a grounding rod, and dispel the charge so it lands in your sentences. Your writing can hold the energy of these forbidden topics.

There are many obstacles to writing about difficult subjects. It's easier to not go there. As you begin to write about them, your mind and body will speak up to let you know you've hit their perceived limit. Their signals will increase in intensity as you get closer and closer. Keep going.

Think of writing about difficult subjects like a challenging ski run: the journey up the mountain in the ski lift is thrilling. The scenery is beautiful and you're comfortably seated, but this is just preparation. The real challenge—and reward—comes when you push off at the top and navigate the steep slopes of your story.

Whenever you start to write what you're most afraid to write—the truths you don't think you can express, scenes you haven't seen in print anywhere else—your heart starts to beat a bit faster. It knows you're about to ski down a daunting hill, and it's on guard for you.

This is writing as a double black diamond run.

And when your skis glide to a stop at the end of the run, you feel exhilarated, calm, and endorphin-laced. Your fears—the voices that told you not to go for it—they disappear.

As you practise writing the forbidden, you come to see your fear in a different way. In some moments, you'll recognize that it's actually *calling* you to the most intense trail. Your fear vibrates with energy that you can use to charge your writing. The next time the call comes to drop into the unknown, you feel more ready. Because you've done this before. You know that the call means you have something true to write.

Writing about the forbidden, or the hidden, or the unsavoury, unseemly, or dark, might not be palatable, intelligible, comforting, or sellable. It might be ugly. It might be something that nobody has ever seen before. It might be something your family won't recognize. It might scare people, or make them sad, or turn them on.

That's okay. Writing is an exploration of what it means to be human, so let yourself explore. Your words may give a reader access to an emotion or an insight that expands their understanding of being alive.

*

ACCEPT THE FEAR OF BEING SEEN

As writers, we often focus on the craft of writing without considering what happens after publication. There is a new level of public exposure that comes with being a published author—showing up at events, being interviewed, and having your work and persona known to readers. This can be a challenging shift for many writers, especially introverts who are used to working in solitude. We want our work to be published, and at the same time, we may also have valid fears about this visibility.

Sometimes, before you start your writing practice, it helps to acknowledge this fear. Instead of avoiding the emotion or trying to make it go away, let yourself feel afraid.

Feel afraid of how your memoir might sound to your family and friends.

Feel afraid of what your colleagues might think if they knew you were writing a romance.

Feel afraid of what your story might reveal about you and aspects of your shadow self.

Feeling your own fear means accepting your emotions without judgment. This can actually help dissolve the emotions. Once released, the neurochemistry of an emotion lasts for about fifteen seconds in your body, give or take. If you feel an emotion for longer than that, it's because your thoughts keep triggering new releases of chemicals to keep you feeling that way. This may happen unconsciously, but with intention we can consciously change our thinking and our brain chemistry.

Accept your fear, and once you can do so, give yourself compassion and understanding. This will release a new blend of neurochemicals; see if you can detect a shift in your mood. Show yourself some kindness. Pour yourself a cup of tea, make a soft nest of blankets on the couch, or call a good friend. Nurturing yourself after facing fear can strengthen your resilience and reinforce your supportive thought patterns, leading to a refreshed emotional state.

It's worth mentioning that if your fear of visibility is very intense, accepting it might not clear it. If your fearful thoughts don't shift when you give them attention and respect, get support.

Fear of visibility can manifest in many emotional and physical ways. Some authors worry about negative reviews or public criticism of their work, while others fear unwanted attention or invasion of privacy. There are also concerns about being misunderstood or having one's words taken out of context. These anxieties can trigger physiological responses that may not have an obvious explanation at first. Sleep disturbances, changes in appetite, fatigue, and an inability to write could all be clues of an underlying fear response to increased visibility. Recognizing these signs is the first step in addressing and overcoming this common challenge.

Photographer and visibility coach Danielle Cohen specializes in this work. She teaches people how to discern the difference between the voice of their inner critic and that of their inner predator. While the first is a benevolent protector who warns you when you're taking a risk and leaving your comfort zone, the second is a destructive internalized belief that wants to separate you from the collective writing community and your potential readers, causing harm to your creative work and career. I encourage you to look up Danielle's teachings and practices for more detail.

It sounds simple, but anyone who has learned how to genuinely feel and face their own fear and come out the other side knows that doing so takes an inordinate amount of courage and practice. Fear of visibility is very real! Sometimes it can be so intense that we emotionally disengage just to get through our writing, or we avoid writing altogether for long periods of time.

Confronting your fear head-on can be transformative in both challenging and positive ways. While it may initially feel uncomfortable, facing your fear of visibility often leads to increased confidence, a stronger connection with your audience, and new opportunities for growth as a writer. It allows you to fully embrace your role as an author and share your work more authentically.

And as a bonus, as you learn how to accept and work through your fear, your emotional capacity will expand, which gives you greater perspective and more range in your writing.

*

PAUSE BEFORE
PUBLISHING

My coaching practice attracts many writers who've already tasted success but are hungry to understand the interplay between intuition and artistic growth. In a memorable session, Lauren, an award-winning essayist I was coaching in writing and blogging, approached me with a dilemma about her latest piece. She had tried something different in her latest blog post and was hesitating before publishing it. She said she'd written something raw and real, and wondered if she should send it to her readers. Was it any good? Could I take a look?

I love Lauren's writing, so I read it right away. This piece was remarkable; it pulsed with an energy I hadn't seen in her work before. It was beautifully unrestrained, moving, intense, vulnerable, and real. I sensed a mix of excitement and unease in Lauren's voice. To help her make a grounded decision about sharing it, I asked her a series of questions and gave her some writing prompts to help her clarify her motivations for writing it.

As we talked, Lauren began to realize that she was drawing from a deeper part of her creativity than she'd accessed before. The piece had emerged from a place where her conscious knowledge about craft and her unconscious inspiration were working together. She told me that she'd written it in a flow state and was surprised by much of what she'd written when she read it the next day. It was full of colourful metaphors, fascinating non sequiturs, and beautiful and unsettling connections she hadn't consciously planned.

Through our session, Lauren understood that this piece represented a significant shift in her writing. She was now creating work that was more powerful and innovative than she'd ever expected of herself. This piece was a nutrient-packed writing sprout, full of potential—and possibly a new direction for her craft and her voice as a writer.

She realized she needed time to fully grasp this evolution in her work. Before sharing it with the world, she wanted to settle into this new version of herself—a writer capable of producing this edgy, strange, and delightful prose. This piece wasn't just another blog post; it was a creative turning point, and Lauren's intuition told her that it deserved time and space to fully develop.

When you write something from a flow state, it arises from a deep place of non-judgment. It's where you can write without eyeing the finished product, whether that's a scene, a story, a book, or a blog post. This unrestricted creative space is special and necessary for writers to occupy.

Waiting to publish can be part of the natural process of settling and evolving as a writer. Like sediment in a riverbed that gets stirred up when you wade through it, our thoughts and emotions can be unsettled after intense creative work. Giving ourselves time allows everything to settle and leaves us with clearer insight and a deeper understanding of what we've created.

If you're on a productivity track or an acceptance track—collecting and counting comments, likes, subscriptions, follows, shares, and publications—it can be extra-difficult for you to hang out in this space of uncertainty.

After we write something, part of us wants to know right away if it's any good or not. That's why we reread what we write—to evaluate it. I learned through experimentation that it's much better for me to read my own writing at least one or two days after I write it. Once I've forgotten the details, I can see it with kinder eyes and a clearer head. Consider experimenting with your own sharing threshold.

Notice if you feel compelled to publish your writing online right away. What's motivating your rush? Of course you get a dopamine hit from pressing that Publish button. It's so satisfying to anticipate (and receive) external validation. But thoughtlessly publishing can be a powerful and justifiable extension of your own inner critic's worst fears. It can also be addictive.

If you're usually quick to publish your writing online, ask yourself: Does publishing this piece feel like a gift for people I care about? Or does it make me excited to see how people react (or how many likes I get, or if people unfollow me after I post)? If you aren't sure, you might want to wait before posting to see if you can get clear on your motivation for doing so.

We're so uncomfortable with uncertainty that we'd rather send our vulnerable work out and have it rejected than sit with the woozy feeling of not knowing whether our writing is any good or not.

There's so much value in waiting until you know how you feel about your own work before you share it for feedback. Try sitting in that awkward pause a little longer before hitting the Send/Post button. Give yourself time to rest and digest what you've created and see how it settles. See how *you* settle.

The first few times you produce something new or raw or strange or deeply true from a flow state, what you write might seem brilliant or it might seem ridiculous. You'll want to do something to make the uncertainty about its quality go away. This might not even be conscious: watch yourself and see what you do to counter the feeling.

You might falter and tell yourself that you're not cut out for writing in general. Surely a real writer doesn't feel so discombobulated, so vulnerable, so uncertain. Doesn't a real writer trust when they're in the zone and go on with confidence?

Personally, I don't know any writers who operate that way.

If you're feeling uncertain about something you've written: Welcome! This is what writing feels like.

Over time, sitting with the wooziness will bring you closer and closer to your best writing. If you distract yourself from staying in that uncertain place, you'll miss what it's teaching you. As discomfort passes and you move into curiosity, notice if any insights arise. You might gain clarity on what you really wanted to say but didn't realize you wanted to say, or you might have said something you didn't quite mean. Your writing might be teaching you something important about your current situation. And, if you really pay attention, you'll get a glimpse of what your writing is asking of you.

With practice, the unknown shifts. It becomes less frightening, more exhilarating. The moment you recognize that sharing your work is a way to stop that fear is the signal for you to hold on a bit more. Wait until the fire of your uncertainty burns down into a bed of coals you can work with. Now you have the opportunity to incorporate any new revelations and make the piece even better.

When we say, "I don't know what to do," it's often a sign that our conscious mind isn't communicating clearly with our unconscious mind. Our intuition has the knowledge we seek—we just have to learn to listen to it.

PRACTICE

If you're writing on the edge of your comfort zone and feel uncertain about your next steps, the following practice can help you communicate with your intuition and make decisions that are aligned with your creative energy.

1.   Before you begin, find a quiet place to sit with your bullet journal and pen.

2.   Settle your body and mind by doing an inner focus practice and/or wholeminded state practice (see pages 31 and 33).

3. Choose two or three of the following prompts and free-write on each one for ten minutes:

    - If you were to imagine your ideal reader experiencing this piece, what sensations or emotions would you want them to feel? Describe these feelings.

    - On a scale of one to ten, how aligned does publishing this piece feel with your creative energy right now? What would need to change to bring that number up?

    - If your writing had a voice of its own, what might it be asking of you in this moment? Write a letter to yourself in the voice of your writing. Start with *What I want you to know is…*

    - Visualize yourself one month from now, having published this piece. What does that future version of you know that you don't know yet?

    - If you were to give this piece of writing a colour, what would it be? And what colour would describe how you feel about sharing it right now? Explore the similarities and contrasts between both colours.

    - Imagine you're having a conversation with your inner protector about this piece. What's one thing you'd want to acknowledge and one thing you'd want to respectfully disagree with?

4. After freewriting, review your responses. Notice any patterns or strong feelings that emerge. These insights can

guide your decision about whether to share your work now or give it more time to develop.

*

ENJOYMENT VERSUS PLEASURE

Every August, Ryan and I go on an eight-day canoe trip.

We prepare for this trip carefully, planning our route, meals, and gear. And once we're out on the water, away from wifi and the rest of civilization, we face new challenges every day.

The weather is unpredictable. The portages are muddy, and sometimes unmarked and hard to find. To boil our water for coffee, we need to find dry firewood and birchbark. We have to keep our food safe from bears. We have to keep ourselves safe from bears.

Canoeing is one of the most enjoyable things I do in my life. While I love these trips more than anything, I don't consider these trips vacations. Canoe trips aren't relaxing.

This is also how I feel about writing books. I choose to go on writing adventures, and I know that obstacles, challenges, and risks will come up in every phase. My creative writing is not exactly work, but it's not rest either.

Writing a book requires both deep play and deep focus. That's one of the signature experiences of writing: feeling relaxed and energized at once. Writing a book doesn't feel easy for me, nor does it feel like an unmanageable burden. What is it then? And how should it feel?

This sounds like a riddle, doesn't it? The nature of writing a book appears contradictory. And yet, within this paradox lies a deep truth about the writing process: that it can be useful to delineate a separation between pleasure and enjoyment.

Pleasure is the contentment we feel when our expectations are met: think of a full belly after a great meal. On a day off, sipping a cool drink and watching waves lap against the shore, my mind is often loose and unfocused. It's a delicious, pleasurable feeling to let my edges softly melt away.

Enjoyment is more complex. My enjoyment of writing requires focused concentration. Though it sounds counterintuitive, experiencing total creative absorption requires discipline. I'm in a trance, but I feel clear and sharp. My edges are crisp.

In his in-depth research on the flow state, psychologist Mihaly Csikszentmihalyi discovered that people find enjoyment in the space between boredom and anxiety.

I love canoeing because, as I paddle silently across the lake for hours and hours, I go into a trance. This is the edge of boredom. And because the wind could pick up at any moment, whitecaps could form on the waves, and my boat could flip, canoeing also happens to set me on the edge of anxiety. I crave the state that exists in the middle of these extremes: as my paddle rhythmically slices into the waves, my peripheral vision takes in the land formations on either side of me. I work to get my bearings as I consult my map, trying to calculate where the next campsite will be and how long it will take us to get there. I search the sky for clues about the weather system that's moving in. Doing all of this at once is peak enjoyment for me and it requires my concentration.

The search for enjoyment is a crucial part of your creative journey. Where are your edges? Find that space where interest meets healthy challenge—where you're stretched but not strained. Start writing there.

In your writing life, you'll grow and your creative questions will change. You may have cracked the code on how to write subtext into your dialogue, but now you want to tackle exploring the omniscient point of view. Or maybe you've written a lot of smart, funny personal essays, but now you want to write a fantasy series for young adults.

Pay special attention to your edges in your writing practice. Where do you find pleasure, and where do you find the most enjoyment?

*

MAGIC SCENES

When you write your best scenes, do you ever find yourself thinking, *Well, that just came out of nowhere.*

It might happen like this: You're trying to work on a new story. You have trouble prioritizing your writing time, until you finally sit down and write for ten minutes. It's not a lot, but at least you've started.

The next day, you sit down again, and it's a bit easier. You write for ten minutes, but then you start to feel that what you're writing isn't very good.

A few days go by, and you continue to write a bit each day. You're starting to feel less self-conscious. The scenes are coming more easily.

Then one day you write something that surprises you. Let's say it's a scene that takes place in a courtroom; the character wears gold ballet flats and has an intriguing accent. What? You don't know why you wrote it. You don't know how you wrote it. But you like this scene. You really like it!

Almost immediately, you think: *Who wrote that? It's really good. I don't know where that came from—was that me?*

We can be quick to own our writing when we think it's bad. But as soon as we write something we think is good, we often act like we don't recognize it.

When unfiltered writing makes its way onto the page in front of us, the judging part of our consciousness doesn't even recognize it. It's normally really good with keeping the door locked. How did something whole make it through the filter? It doesn't make sense to our ego.

Writing unselfconsciously can feel like an act of magic, one that surprises even the magician. Scenes arrive in your mind like rabbits popping out of hats. Make no mistake, they are still yours. They just come to you in a different way, like dreams. You don't control your dreams the way you control your workout schedule, your sock drawer, the way you organize your bookshelves. They come organically. You prepare for their arrival by making room for them.

Clear mental space for your unselfconscious writing. Embrace what's outside your control. Practice your magic and cultivate that feeling of surprise.

Make more room for these magic scenes and they will come to you.

*

THE CONFOUNDING WHOLENESS
OF KNOWING EVERYTHING
AT ONCE

When you're writing a novel, you have to learn to tolerate the confounding wholeness that comes from simultaneously knowing your entire story and only pieces of it.

You can only write one word at a time. You gather these words in linear order to form images and scenes, and you carefully arrange these images into a shape that you hope makes sense. As the writer, you hold the entire project in your head, and at the same time, you also have to organize the words and sentences, chisel out a clear point of view, fact-check that a timeline makes sense, draw characters who feel like real people, and structure a story to contain whole lives and worlds. This is incredibly complex mental and emotional work.

You also have to do all of this in real time and in real life. Once you close your notebook, all of the relationships, experiences, and challenges awaiting you as a person are right there, and you have to make sense of those, too.

How you create a book and how you create a life follow the same general process: you set out with an intention and move toward resolution. You may hold a vision of an outcome in your mind, but you don't know exactly how to navigate your way there. You pay attention and try to make good decisions. You show up regularly, course-correcting as you go.

Your mind can simultaneously create and inhabit these two distinct realities. Keep in mind that your actual life unfolds at a much slower pace than the one you're crafting in your novel. While your lived experience progresses moment by moment, your fictional world compresses time, leaping across hours, days, or even years in the span of a few paragraphs. This acceleration of events not only keeps readers engaged but also creates a coherent narrative structure. And these vastly different time scales coexist in your mind, requiring cognitive flexibility as you switch between them.

Your creative work demands a lot of thinking, but what you're doing doesn't all happen through thought alone. Writing fiction engages your entire being: your senses create vivid scenes, your intuition guides character development, your proprioception helps you embody your characters' physical experiences, your interoception tunes you into subtle emotional nuances, and your sense of time and chronology weaves the fabric of your narrative. All these elements working in concert can feel overwhelming. That's when you need to shift away from thinking, so you can experience wholeness directly without having to organize it mentally.

PRACTICE

When you feel intellectually overwhelmed by the complexity of your writing project, this exercise will help you experience wholeness without having to "figure it out." By taking an intentional break from thinking, you'll access a sense-connected way of being, a feeling-state that exists without judgment, label, or evaluation. Training yourself to set words apart from your experience helps you become aware of what your body knows without intellectualizing it.

Give yourself twenty minutes for this exercise. For the duration of that time, you get to be yourself the way an animal is always itself. You get to practise just being.

1. Go outside. Leave your phone and any writing tools at home. If possible, find a natural setting with trees, birds, or water. Your backyard, a city park, or a nearby trail will work well.

2. Let go of your writing project, research, and any other mental clutter. Resist the urge to problem-solve or plan your next scene. Try not to even talk to yourself in your head.

3. When you notice yourself thinking in words, gently redirect your attention to your senses. What do you see, hear, smell, or feel?

4. Narrow your focus to small details: the pattern of leaves on a tree, the rhythm of bird calls, the sensation of wind on your skin, or the subtle shades of colour in a flower.

5. If you find yourself getting frustrated or impatient, remind yourself that this is part of the process. Your mind is used to being busy with words and plots. Give it time to settle into a different mode of awareness.

6. Before heading back home, take a moment to notice how you feel. Has your breathing changed? Do you feel more or less energized? Are you more aware of your body?

When you return to your writing, don't rush to capture your experience in words. Instead, allow the sensations and non-verbal awareness to subtly inform your work. You might find that solutions to plot problems or new character insights arise without force.

Remember, in societies that emphasize constant productivity, these deliberate moments of wordless being are crucial for writers. They're not just breaks from writing; they're an essential part of your creative process. By regularly engaging in this practice, you can continue to refill your well of experiencing sensation. Giving yourself time to experience wordlessness is a kindness to your whole self and can lead to fresh inspiration and a renewed connection to your project.

SWITCH GEARS

I used to think writing books was supposed to be hard work and that it was unreasonable to enjoy it. Writers talk about this a lot. "A writer is someone for whom writing is more difficult than it is for other people," Thomas Mann said. "I hate writing. I love having written," said Dorothy Parker.

The implication here is that if it feels fun or smooth and easy, if writing is something that you genuinely want to do with your time, then your work won't be any good.

I've spent too many hours of my life forcing myself to write through resistance instead of pausing to listen to what that resistance was trying to tell me. I've spent years focused on the problem of writing instead of attending to the beauty of creative curiosity, language, and emotion, and the pleasure of using my writing skills to good effect.

Resistance shows up as a myriad of feelings: stuck, sleepy, avoidant, fraught, nauseous, afraid, distracted, or bored. These feelings aren't a problem. They're information.

Most often, your resistance is a valid request from your unconscious mind to take care of yourself. You might need some combination of rest, reflection, friendship, movement, or nourishment. Sometimes resistance signals that you're about to leave your comfort zone and move into rarely visited emotional territory. It can be a warning that you're about to open up a box of big unprocessed feelings or events, and maybe you should find a way to support yourself—like getting a good therapist—before you open that box.

Resistance is not an adversary. It's your unconcious mind sending messages to your conscious self.

Many books on writing and craft teach us that the answer to resistance is to write anyway. *Stay in your chair and triumph will be yours.* Because I believed writing was supposed to feel like a fight, I trained myself to dissociate. This limiting belief left me with two options: to write from a detached perspective or to activate my nervous system with adrenaline so I could slay my resistance like a dragon.

Picture yourself in a cute vintage Fiat 500. It's a standard transmission, and you're not using the clutch properly, but you insist on driving anyway. Dark sounds emanate from the vehicle. Your stomach turns over. You're damaging the car. It's hard work, it feels awful, and you can see that nothing good is coming from it. No one would recommend driving a Fiat in this terrible way.

If it doesn't even work for a car, why should it work for a human being?

What if your writing felt like properly driving the Fiat? What if you listened to the engine, paid attention to the road, and monitored your speed? Your actions would probably make for a smooth and effortless ride. You and the car could work together. The joy of driving lies in intuitively knowing when and how to change gears—and you gain this intuition by paying careful attention.

You don't necessarily want to feel detached and carefree when you're writing. As a writer, you want to feel involved and engaged in your work. But you can still navigate a bumpy road without grinding your gears.

Check in with yourself and be honest about how you're feeling. If you're not enjoying your time spent writing, or if you feel like your gears are jammed—that is, if you're bored, resentful, overwhelmed, stressed out, or numb—stop what you're doing.

Take a short rest. Do nothing for five minutes. Go outside. Drink water. Call a writing friend. Play some music and dance. Have a snack. Take a nap. Interrupt the pattern.

When you're ready to refocus, find one small part of the scene you're writing that makes you feel engaged again—even if it's as tiny as the hot pink shoelace in your character's shoe. Invite your curiosity. What *is* that thing? Describe it.

If you're still struggling with the scene, head to your freewriting notebook to write and reflect. Start with the prompt "I don't want to write about..." or "I am resisting writing because..." and freewrite for several minutes.

When you respect your unconscious mind, your awareness expands. What is your resistance telling you? Pay attention to the information it's providing so you can keep your gears turning smoothly.

✳

SLOW DOWN TO MAKE SENSE

Be the weirdo at the coffee shop: Close your eyes to really focus on the taste of your peppermint tea. Pause to notice the
way the street light illuminates the ice on your windshield,
and take note of the patterns the crystals make. Pay attention
to the texture of traffic sounds until you feel your body make
sense of them. Slip into the feeling of how your body moves
through space. Feel the ground under your feet, the chair under your hips, the air against your skin.

Invite your body into your writing practice and give it time
and space to do what it does best; let your body perceive the
world through your senses. It helps to fully understand and
internalize the feelings in your body in order to properly
transform them into words. As you recognize the contours
of any sensations you try to describe, your conscious mind
can begin to make sense of the clues.

When you invite your body to join your writing, you infuse
more energy into your scenes. You want to tell a story using
all of your tools: your creativity, intuition, intellectual reason-
ing, and the intelligence of your five senses.

As a creative writer, this is a gift you can give to others: you can use language to effectively share an embodied experience. Your sensory engagement allows your reader to be physically present in the scenes you describe. They get to feel like they're right there, living in your story. They can transcend their own reality and truly inhabit the world you've created.

Slowing down to write with your senses deepens your own connection to your characters and story and makes the reading experience more impactful and memorable. As Gord Downie, the renowned Canadian musician and poet, once said, "I write to give people access to their own emotions." By engaging their senses through your writing, you're doing exactly that—offering readers a visceral, embodied experience that connects them to the richness of sensory existence. It's a form of experiential empathy that unlocks their own emotional landscape. You're providing a chance to see, feel, and understand life from another perspective. This is a gift of nourishment for you and your readers.

This isn't just an intellectual process, so don't overthink it. Let it be a whole-minded approach. Experiencing a feeling while simultaneously writing the words to describe the feeling will transmit an essence through time and space. Slow down, invite your body to the page, and let the sensations become the words.

*

IT'S NOT A PROBLEM

I spent one summer revising the final draft of my novel, and by September I had come to the last few chapters. I'd booked myself a writing retreat that month—a Hedgebrook workshop with the author Karen Joy Fowler—in a beautiful location in Tuscany. Karen's genre-blending fiction is one of my biggest influences. It was a wish come true to finish my revision with her guidance.

Midway through the retreat, though, I couldn't sleep. The light of the full moon poured through my room's window, illuminating all my book's potential problems. What if my writing wasn't literary enough? What if the ending was too ambiguous? What if the first-person POV made the protagonist's emotions too strong? What if retyping my draft from scratch was the wrong way to revise it? Had I given my characters the wrong names? Before I sent the manuscript to my agent, I wanted to fix everything I could.

The next morning, I came to class with my list of revision questions. Karen listened to me carefully. Then she asked, "Why are you making your creative decisions into problems?"

Her question interrupted the current of my thinking. The energy in my body shifted—it was like I'd been paddling a river that abruptly changed direction. From this perspective, the whole world looked different. For a moment, I couldn't form a thought. I didn't know how to look at my revisions if I wasn't looking for problems.

I spent about forty-five minutes stunned and disoriented. Then I went back to my desk focused on decision-making instead of problem-solving. I spent the final days of the retreat making creative choices that felt fun and interesting. I finished the draft later that fall and it was published the following spring.

When you start writing a book, it can feel like swimming in a big, deep lake. The expanse of infinite uncertainty can be overwhelming and make you feel small—but it can also be liberating and exciting. You can navigate that abundance of creative possibility by setting a timer or a word count. This puts a temporary cap on endlessness, and the structure frees you to stay open and curious as you write.

As you get closer to finishing your project, the choices you make begin to limit that expansiveness. That abundance of creative possibility narrows, and the lake funnels into a stream. The water is moving faster now, and you gain momentum as you write. At this point, you have new opportunities to make creative and strategic decisions.

The flow is not a problem. Recognizing how the flow moves is the important part. Let your energy shift to match where you are in your story. Approach the changes you're considering openly and with flexibility. Your state of mind is at its best when it's calm, creative, and curious.

Commit to your creative decisions and see them through. You're writing a story, not analyzing data. The "correctness" of your choices comes from your state of mind. Trust yourself.

How do you know if one scene should happen before another one, for instance? Or if the story should be told in first person or third person? Or if the main character should be named Jules instead of Harrison? Or whether you've got the right title for your book? The only way to know is for you to make a decision about it.

Finding the right title for your novel is not a problem you have to solve—it's a choice you get to make. To finish your book, you're going to make many decisions that go one way and not the other way. You're going to keep narrowing and focusing and deciding until you resolve all the loose ends.

What kind of writer would you be if you trusted your decisions?

What if you decided that the third-person point of view was right and then just went for it?

Decided that there would be two sisters instead of three?

Decided to tell your story non-chronologically, using flashbacks and time jumps?

Decided to put elements of magical realism into your otherwise realistic narrative?

Every book written is the result of a writer's self-appointed authority to make decisions and to trust that those decisions are the best ones. There's no secret set of instructions; writing and storytelling are about making decisions and living with them. There's no need to worry about the things you can control.

*

CONNECT WITH THANKS

Writing is an often thankless and solitary pursuit, especially while you're in the process of a first draft. You're alone with your thoughts to navigate self-doubt and uncertainty. But if you keep writing anyway, something remarkable happens: you improve. You learn how to dissolve the force field that tries to keep you from your desk. There are seasons and phases where you show up to write every day. Eventually, you build a practice—a practice rooted in perseverance and, perhaps, something deeper. Gratitude.

Gratitude can be a powerful source of inspiration. On the tough days when it feels harder to show up, you might find comfort reading the books that have kept you on track before. For me, those books include *The Book of Form and Emptiness* by Ruth Ozeki, *Son of a Trickster* by Eden Robinson, and *Weetzie Bat* by Francesca Lia Block. These stories remind me why I write and ground me in the magic of storytelling. I'm grateful to these authors—returning to their work fuels my own creativity.

Gratitude, however, isn't just about what we receive. It's about recognizing the interconnectedness of creative energy.

As writers, we're not alone in our pursuits. The books that inspire us are connected to the creative source we bring to our writing. Creative energy is an unlimited resource, and each story we write contributes to the collective force of human creativity.

Imagine one of your favourite authors. They sit at their desk day after day, managing writing alongside life's other demands—just like you. They may face different challenges, like difficult reviews or uneven book sales, but the creative journey is the same.

Remember: All creative endeavours are interconnected and dynamic. The gifts we receive as readers are connected to the gifts we give as writers. When you reread the books and authors you love the most, you are primed to tap into creative energy; in turn, your own writing adds to this shared creative force and keeps it in motion.

One way to embody this sense of connection is through the act of giving thanks. I learned this powerful writing practice from author Carolyn See. It was so life-changing that I now assign it to every class I teach. If an author's work has moved you, thank them. You share the same tools, the same struggles, and you've likely read many of the same books. A personal note is a generous way to say, "Your work is meaningful to me."

Your appreciation of certain writing can make room for more creative energy in your own writing. Writing a thank-you card to an author isn't just a kind gesture—it's a practice that strengthens your connection to the craft and can deepen your sense of belonging within the writing community. Gratitude keeps you on track and shifts your mindset from one of isolation to one of appreciation and participation. This practice is a simple, powerful way to create that shift.

PRACTICE

If your favourite author is still living, now is the perfect time to send them a note of thanks. And even if they have passed, the act of writing the note can still be transformative for you. You never know what shifts might occur in your creative energy once you release that gratitude into the world.

Most writers don't receive heaps of fan mail the way actors and celebrities do. It's probable that your note will reach the author directly, and that your words of gratitude will affect them. I always like to send a thank-you note after someone gives me an important gift. Especially when the gift has changed my life—something books can do.

Here's how to do it: Make your note simple and sincere. You could write something like "Thank you for writing [book title]. I loved it!" I like to use a flat card, like a postcard, so I'm not tempted to ramble. Remember, this is just a thank-you. This is about momentum, not exchange. Expect no response.

Choose nice paper or a card, a good pen, and a stamp that feels thoughtful. If the author has a website, you can often find a mailing address on their contact page. Otherwise, send your card care of the author's agent or publisher.

Once you've sent the note, pay attention to how you feel. You may notice a renewed sense of creative purpose or a deeper connection to your role as a writer within the larger literary ecosystem.

IMAGINE THE WILD RABBIT

Creative journeys include obstacles that might be formidable and intense. How you approach these obstacles can make a difference in the outcome. Facing challenges head-on might push you outside your comfort zone, which can be necessary to help you move on to the next part of your writing project. One way to do this is to set deadlines. Deadlines provide constructive tension, and consistency is important for any creative endeavour. So yes: Set a schedule and stick to it. Track your writing progress and celebrate your accomplishments.

At the same time, remember to invite creative curiosity into your process. Tune into your powers of receptivity just as much as you tune into inspired action.

You don't want to start banging out your writing practice only because you Must. Check. It. Off. List. Your creative curiosity is not a chore. If you're a determined and dogged type of person, if you know you can override your body's needs in order to get a task done, if you feel validated by how hard you can work, it's a good idea to check in with yourself once or twice a day to reconnect to your creative curiosity. At the same time, discipline is not a dirty word. You need both the softness of curiosity and steady rigour to establish the balance that will propel you and your writing forward.

Take a deep breath. Imagine your creative curiosity as a wild cottontail rabbit. Its whiskers twitch in the cool air. It can sense safety. It can sense danger, and it will dart away if it feels heavy vibrations in the ground. You can change your state to show your curiosity that your discipline isn't a threat. Exhale to release the tension in your chest and belly. Let your shoulders drop. Make your creative curiosity feel welcome.

Receptivity brings ease, which can then make your writing life more sustainable. A more relaxing, nourishing practice has a better chance of bringing out richness in your writing and prevents burnout.

PRACTICE

This exercise is a good way to check in with yourself when you're in a writing-is-a-grind mindset. Its goal is to move you back toward welcoming your creative curiosity, cultivating your receptivity, and reconnecting you to what you love about writing.

1. Pay attention to the signs of your own doggedness. How does your body feel when it's under pressure? What texture and speed is your breath? How do your thoughts show up as physical sensations? How are you holding your jaw? Do your eyes feel dry? Are your shoulders tight? Notice your own physiology.

2. Name whatever it is you notice. For example: *I feel tight-ness in my chest.*

3. Ask yourself why this feeling is here now. You don't have to know or find the answer; just ask the open-ended question. Genuinely wondering about it will activate your curiosity. It literally helps to say this aloud or in your head: *Hmm… I wonder why this feeling is here now?*

4. Make space to rebalance your creative energy by free-writing in your journal. Set a timer for ten minutes and respond to one or more of these prompts below without censoring or editing yourself.

   I love writing because…

   What I love about being a writer is…

   When I resist writing, it's because…

   I feel whole when…

   My writing wants me to…

Write by hand. Let your handwriting get messy. Your willingness to be vulnerable is a signal of safety to your creative curiosity.

It might be helpful to answer a single prompt several times in a row. This can help to break through your surface thoughts and lead to deeper insights from your creative unconscious.

*

TIME IS MADE OUT OF REST

Rest is not a waste of time, it's the way you make time.

Rest should be the foundation of your writing life. Move your attention toward it. Take naps. Stare out the window into middle space. Act as though you have all the time in the world to write your book.

Actually tell yourself: *I have so much time.*

When you're well-rested, connections between ideas or images may become clearer. You have better ideas. You're replenished and feel more sane. You might use your skills in more interesting ways, with more care and thought. This makes you more effective, efficient, and resilient.

Rest makes you a better writer.

Productivity is irrelevant when you're in a whole-minded state. A milkweed pod does not tell itself it has value because it completes its task of releasing seeds. A piece of granite does not believe that if it does good work now, it can rest later.

Their state of *being* and their state of *doing* are the same.

If writing doesn't feel like your state of doing and your state of being have merged, it might be time to take a rest.

*

TRACK YOUR PROGRESS

When you emerge from a creative trance, it can be hard to tell if anything you've done is worthwhile. This can feel disorienting at best, and at worst, demoralizing.

I know writers who go away on a retreat, write every day, fill pages in their notebooks, transcribe their work, and still come home feeling dissatisfied, convinced that their time away was fruitless because they haven't yet finished their book.

Depending on how you want to engineer your creative life, writing a book might take you anywhere from eight months to ten years from start to finish. So if your goal is to finish writing a book, you need to know how to break that goal down into measurable steps and trackable quotas. This will help to convince the logical, evaluating side of your mind that you're making great progress through the deeply creative but not always linear process of writing.

The creative process is so dynamic that when you lock yourself into a quota—say, a certain number of pages per day every day for three months—you might not give your creative work enough space to evolve. Your well-laid plans might backfire and instead limit your creative progress.

How do you set an achievable quota, measure your progress, and still remain flexible and open to change as your story evolves? You can track your progress in three different ways.

Some days, track by word count

When you have a plan and you want motivation to stick to it, it's great to set a target to write a certain number of words and pages. When I'm working on a book-length project, I aim for a thousand words a day. Some days I only get to six hundred words, and some days I hit two thousand. It averages out in a way I find satisfying. And the pages really do add up; it feels great to see your completed pages in the "done" pile. This is one of the most obvious ways to convince yourself of your progress, because the output is visible proof of time spent writing.

I like to track my pages and try to reach my word-count quotas for at least one full week at a time. This lets me benefit from the momentum of a daily routine.

The quantity of your writing does not ensure the quality of your state of mind, though. It's possible to dissociate and detach from your creative curiosity just to meet your writing quota. This is why you should track your progress in two other ways: to nurture your progress and the presence that brings magic to your writing.

Some days, track by time

Writing freely within a time container can be more useful than counting your output. When you're ideating, generating new work, redeveloping your practice after some time away, or planning a structure or outline, I find it best to count the minutes and hours spent writing.

Time tracking is useful mid-project, too, for puzzling out plots, exploring character backgrounds and settings, and generating new scenes for a revision.

Count your hours and minutes when you want to honour writing-adjacent activities like mind-mapping, reading, researching, and rearranging timelines. I like to set up my daily freewriting practice in thirty-minute chunks. In those, I write continuously without concern for grammar or structure, and use prompts to stimulate ideas. When I'm exploring story structure, plot, and character development, I like having more time to think about how different parts of the story fit together, so I write in ninety-minute chunks.

If you write for more than ninety minutes a day, do your brain a favour and take a break between your scheduled blocks of time to reset. You'll come back to your writing more focused.

Some days, track by insights

When your writing feels like it's stalled, start tracking your insights. This can get you moving again.

There's an important synergy that occurs between creative output and rest. Your writing process needs white space, too, and tending it makes room for surprises and synchro-nicities to arise. Build insight tracking into your project plans so you can better recognize these accomplishments as progress, too.

There are times when you need to go for a long walk to think about that really weird dream you had, or maybe you're watching a movie with your kids and see a plot twist in the film that shows you how to solve your story's puzzle. Or you order a new smoothie flavour at your local café and you sud-denly understand that your antagonist is allergic to strawber-ries! This kind of stuff happens when you're writing a book. Make room for it.

Keep track of your daily insights and learnings in your bullet journal, even on days when you don't make a word count or a time count. This becomes documentation of your writing work. I start a new page in my bullet journal to use for insight tracking every month. It's a dated log of my insights, so even when I don't write for an hour or meet my word-count quota on that particular day, I have a record of the creative work I did do. I learned the value of tracking my insights from au-thor Jill Margo, who learned it from author Susan Swan. It's a game-changer.

Aim to incorporate all three tracking modes into your pro-cess. While the balance between word count, time, and in-sights may shift depending on your project's phase and your personal needs, consistently using this trio of tracking meth-ods will give you a well-rounded view of your progress and nurture both your productivity and creativity.

＊

I DON'T KNOW HOW
TO TASTE THIS

When we encounter something new and different, deciding not to like it is one easy way out of the experience.

Another approach is to engage with the newness. This is where cultivating curiosity is essential. If you can stay open to possibility for long enough, something interesting happens: your imagination comes alive.

By shifting our mindset from avoidance to curiosity, we open ourselves to new experiences and insights. Instead of shutting down, we start to explore. Chef and Michelin-starred restaurateur Pim Techamuanvivit offers a cue on how to reframe our thinking, and I love this quote: "In Thai, when we eat something that's not to our taste, we don't really say, 'I don't like this' or 'this is bad.' We say, 'I don't know how to eat this.'"

What a difference this subtle shift in thinking makes. Instead of *I don't like this feeling*, it's *I don't know how to be with this feeling.*

Embracing curiosity is a skill used regularly by creative people. Our natural inclination toward curiosity and fascination can be deliberately strengthened. What might become possible for us if we engage our creative curiosity more often and for longer stretches of time? Opportunities to do this exist everywhere:

What flavours are confusing to your palate?

What kinds of conversations make your head spin?

What ways of moving your body feel foreign and strange?

What views and perspectives disorient you?

What story structures are unfamiliar and hard to understand?

Remind yourself that learning how to tolerate the new is more useful and more powerful than fearing discomfort. Your job is to pay attention and learn while you absorb different experiences—what you do like and what you don't like, what you know how to do and don't, what you gravitate toward or move away from. This is how you calibrate your tastes as a writer.

Pay attention to what you "don't know how to eat" in your writing—whether that's personal memory or history, fantasy or futurities. Embrace these unknowns as opportunities for exploration—try writing something in a way you've never before written, and enjoy the new neural pathways you build as your capacity for exploring new experiences increases.

*

USE YOUR BODY

Your body's wisdom makes it possible for you to know things fully. When you're writing, you use your mind and body together to fully access your senses: What is it like to suck on a cinnamon candy, to pick up a squirming child, to step on a wooden deck with your bare feet?

When you're sitting for hours curled over your notebook or keyboard, lost in the world of your book, it's easy to forget that your body is still living and breathing in the real world. Sometimes we focus so much on what's happening in our heads that we might forget that our minds need our bodies to move.

You aren't just a big brain on a stick: you're an embodied creature. We all are. Regular physical activity improves cognitive function and enhances attention, memory, and processing speed. Not only will movement help you read and write more clearly—and heighten your attention to details like flavours and colours—but the delicious mix of hormones triggered by exercise also makes you feel good. Endorphins reduce pain and bring feelings of euphoria, dopamine is associated with reward and pleasure, and serotonin plays a role in mood regulation. All to say, it's definitely worth it to incorporate regular movement into your writing life.

We also get a temporary testosterone boost from exercise, especially resistance training and high-intensity interval training (HIIT). This rise lasts for about fifteen minutes to an hour after exercise and can bring on feelings of confidence and assertiveness, which help us be more brave and more decisive in our writing. Use that boost when writing scenes that require your characters to show up in difficult and dramatic situations, and when you need to believe that you can write them through their conflict and into resolution.

Your body has awareness that is not connected to thinking. Shake it and dance it. Stretch your muscles. Lift heavy things. Make your heart race. Sweat. Wiggle. Use your body! Appreciate it and spend quality time with it—movement is a tool to balance the brain and the body.

PRACTICE

Energize your body and mind to dial up more of your creative courage. This exercise combines physical movement with a writing challenge to help you push your boundaries and access new levels of creativity.

Give yourself about thirty minutes for this exercise: ten minutes for physical activity and twenty minutes for writing.

Choose a short, intense physical activity that gets your heart racing and your body moving. This could be a quick HIIT workout, a set of burpees, jumping jacks, or a brief run. The goal is to get your blood pumping and those feel-good hormones flowing. (If exercise really isn't your thing, and you have any pre-existing conditions, take it slow or talk to your doctor first.)

After two to three minutes of exercise, take a moment to catch your breath and centre yourself. Notice how your body feels—the increased heart rate, the warmth in your muscles, the surge of energy. Keep moving for seven more minutes, resting and recalibrating as needed.

Now, sit down with your writing materials. Choose a project or scene that you've been hesitant to tackle—something that feels risky or challenging. This could be an emotionally charged scene, a controversial topic, or a style of writing you've never attempted before.

For the next twenty minutes, write without censoring yourself. Feel the strength and confidence you've just experienced in your body during the exercise, and let the physical energy from your workout fuel your creativity. Let yourself be bolder, more honest, or more experimental than you usually allow yourself to be.

This practice combines the benefits of physical activity—including the temporary boost in testosterone and confidence—with the challenge of tackling a writing project. By linking these experiences, you're training your mind and body to associate the feelings of physical empowerment with creative courage. Over time, this can help you approach your writing with more confidence and willingness to take risks.

BORDER-COLLIE MIND

It was my first morning back home after a week visiting my family in Indiana. I hadn't made time for my writing practice during my visit, and as a result my mind had grown noisy with thoughts. They went something like this:

It's raining! Oh no, that will make the peonies droopy.

Yeah, but the garden does need the water...

When I was in Indiana, the birds woke us up before dawn. I'm still so tired.

Ugh, the bathroom really needs to be cleaned. But I don't have time to do it!

I really wish I could talk to Cath. Should I call her today? I want to call her. No, I'm sure she's too busy to talk.

This is a truncated list. All these thoughts came in an instant, and each new thought replaced the last seamlessly, like links in a chain.

My mind is like a border collie. When I don't give it work to do, it gets restless and into trouble. But when I put it out in a field with some sheep to herd (that is, get a notebook and a pen and start to write), I can turn all of those active, non-stop, sometimes anxious thoughts into sentences and then into stories.

Writing gives my border-collie mind a job to do. And having an important job can create focus and help me to write with creative curiosity. This state of mind turns my manic thought energy into fertile material.

I write about a garden in the rain, or cleaning my bathroom, or birds in the morning, or calling Cath to say hi. I write about the same stuff I was thinking about. But when I write this all intentionally, with curiosity, everything changes.

When you feel overwhelmed by your active mind, deliberately shift your attention from the content of your thoughts to the energy your thoughts are creating. Become an electrician: tap your wiring into the flow of this electricity and use the energy to light up your writing.

I say this like it's an easy thing to do, but I know it's not easy. It takes practice and training. Be nice when you catch yourself in a thought-chain fever. Your mind is a border collie, remember? Super-smart, super-cute. You're in puppy training! Remind yourself that your mind is telling stories and making up pictures and movies—lots of mind-pictures and lots of mind-movies.

These mind-movies are your raw materials. You're a writer, which means you have a natural ability to create and make patterns out of ideas. Study and practice will further develop these skills. Work with your border-collie mind to keep it healthy, satisfied, and proud to do the work it was born to do.

Once you've separated your awareness from the content of your thoughts, you'll stop feeling so harassed by the internal noise. Now you can zero in on what you're going to write. That could look something like this:

It's raining! Oh no, that will make the peonies droopy.

Write about heavy, soggy flower heads dipping down toward the wet grass.

Yeah, but the garden does need the water...

Write about dry ground drenched with water, the grass perky and green, a fresh scent in the air.

When I was in Indiana, the birds woke us up before dawn. I'm still so tired.

Write about the big oak tree in the backyard, cool and fresh midnight-blue air, how the chirping robins sound in the dark.

Ugh, the bathroom really needs to be cleaned. But I don't have time to do it!

Write about yellow rubber gloves, a jar of Borax, the dull film over the faucet wiped away with a pink cloth.

I really wish I could talk to Cath. Should I call her today? I want to call her. No, I'm sure she's too busy to talk.

Write about the deep sound of her voice, the way she slices green onions, the last four digits of her phone number, her coral jumpsuit.

Channel your anxious thoughts into a form of appreciation for details. Some of us are keenly visual people and we see pictures in our mind's eye most often; others focus on the tactile sensations of touch; and still others are primarily auditory and tune into dialogue, voices, or sounds. Whatever your default thinking mode, remind yourself to pay attention to the quality of your thinking rather than the content of your thoughts. As you learn to guide your border-collie mind with gentle intention, you'll find it becomes an eager and loyal companion, ready to herd your thoughts into vibrant and satisfying fields.

*

RITUAL

I once took a break from writing for a few months to refill my well and gain new perspective on my novel-in-progress. When I returned to my early-morning practice, I felt ready to write the third act. My commitment to write in the morning felt familiar, and it also felt completely different that time around.

My motivations shifted during my time off. Writing the first two acts of this story changed me in subtle ways, and I recognized shifts in some of my curiosities, interests, and observations about people.

I marked this change by clearing the windowsill in my office. I removed the old talismans I had gathered when I started writing the first draft of my new novel—an unpolished chunk of quartz, an acorn, and several pine cones—and I scattered them in the woods, back where they came from. There was space on the sill for new talismans, or maybe I'd choose to keep it open and spacious.

For this new start, I also cleaned the surface of my writing desk. I was geekily excited to use my new tools (dark pink

ink, a blue-and-gold blank notebook). This was not avoidance. I wasn't procrastinating.

This is part of my process: my version of deep contemplation sometimes looks like cleaning, clearing, and rearranging. I spend a good chunk of time considering paper texture and ink colour before starting this next phase of my writing because I know that everything offers meaning. The paper and ink themselves are metaphors for the project, in a way that language can't fully capture. I want the feeling of the paper to align with the feeling of the story. I want the colour and consistency of my ink to harmonize with the tone of my writing. I'm wired that way. I'm weird that way.

To be clear, all of this careful pondering and object-placing doesn't directly make my writing better. I like the ritual because it helps me feel more purposeful about choices that are otherwise arbitrary. Deliberately choosing pink ink to match the emotional tone for my book makes me more confident and prepared to write. When the texture of the paper feels right, I know I'm on the right track and I'm motivated to keep writing. This helps make the impossible seem more possible.

Designing your own rituals can help with creative decision-making. Magical thinking is an appropriate technique for writers to embrace—after all, writing a book is itself a form of magic.

*

ONE STONE AND NOT
THE OTHER

One of my most memorable writing teachers, the poet and translator Peter Levitt, taught me to pay attention to my mind when I walked down the beach. When you pick up stones from the beach, he asked, what are you doing? What makes you pick up one stone and not the other one? What's happening in your mind as you make those choices?

Writers are always making a series of unconscious decisions based on what feels right. Why this word and not this other one? You think some things through rationally, but your best creative decisions may seem arbitrary and unexplainable. And yet with each stone you select, each word you choose, you're making a creative commitment.

Some of the writers I teach keep projects on a wait list. They have lots of ideas they want to pursue, and they often ask me how they know which one to write next. The truth is, you choose your projects the same way you choose your words, using a combination of intellect and intuition: you think about it, you check in with the unexplainable, and eventually you make a creative commitment to go for it, or you don't.

Every stone on the beach is an interesting stone. There are no duds—but there are some that genuinely fascinate you more than others. You get to decide where you put your attention. You don't have to explain or defend your choices to anyone.

Think about the writing projects on your list. Consider your current capacity by measuring your time, your energy, your resources. Then let yourself walk down the beach to see what you notice about what you notice.

Right now, I have four writing projects on the go: this book that you're reading right now, an idea for a second volume, an idea for a TV show, and the finished draft of a novel to revise. I have a hunch about what I might want to do next, but I haven't made a commitment yet. There's more beach walking I want to do first.

PRACTICE

When you don't know what to write next, freewrite answers to these open-ended questions in your bullet journal. Continue repeatedly as needed, ideally before bed or in the morning, when your brain is more receptive:

- Where does my energy meet my desire?

- Which project feels like the most fun?

- What am I obsessed with right now?

- What gives me energy when I think about writing it?

- Who will I become after I write my next project?

Taking time to reflect on these questions gives your unconscious mind an opportunity to offer you answers. At some point you'll be ready to commit to one project and to set the others aside for later.

If this process feels too ungrounded for you, give yourself a decision deadline. This adds a bit of (hopefully) useful pressure. A good time limit for reflection might be a week to a month (or longer, if you're recovering from creative decision fatigue).

By choosing a project, you're bringing it into existence, giving it life and form. This act of decision is a powerful creative force—it's the moment when countless possibilities crystallize into a specific path. Your commitment breathes life into that one idea, allowing it to grow and evolve through your creative energy.

You don't have to rush your decision. Trust this process. Trust your intuition. There's power in making a creative choice and standing by it. This power belongs to you.

✳

LOVE YOUR CHARACTERS

Writing real characters who have hopes, fears, passions, and secrets requires your genuine emotional investment with no promise of return. It's much easier to just write a story about stuff that happens, with scenes and people with names and jobs walking around in two dimensions.

Character work is partly about the art of creating composites from a bed of real detail. Like when you notice the way the cashier you just met paints her nails, the fussy way your mother walks her dog, or the odd way your high school teacher pronounces the word *apricot*, and you put all of those things into one person and name her Frenchie. You've now created a character.

When you throw in a want or need and a secret—say Frenchie had a son when she was sixteen, gave him up for adoption, and believes she has recently found him working at a library in Whistler, British Columbia—you have drama. Done!

Except that Frenchie doesn't quite have the power to come alive off the page. She has specific qualities, but she isn't real.

She will only become real with love.

Remember the children's story *The Velveteen Rabbit*? That's the kind of love I'm talking about: the love a child has for a stuffed animal. This is not romantic love; this is imagination powered by emotion. It's the creative play you use to make non-sentient things feel alive. You do this when you use a hand to make a wool sock speak as a puppet: you suspend your disbelief and imagine that there is a sentient being talking to you. It's Sock.

You bring Sock to life by pretending and feeling at the same time. When your imagination is powered by your emotion, your heart lights up. It doesn't matter what the emotion is— it could be funny or scary, whimsical or dramatic. If you have an audience, they'll feel it as soon as you start, and then you all get to share the delight of being in the presence of Sock.

When you remove the wool sock from your hand, you may spend a moment feeling sad about the loss of Sock. That split second when a deep part of you looks at the wool expectantly, as though waiting for it to come to life again—that's the love that made Sock real. To cast this kind of spell, you have to connect your heart to the imaginary being you've created. To break the spell, you have to disconnect your heart.

Writing characters is deeper work than most people expect, because most people stopped playing with their stuffed animals when they were little. Opening our adult-sized hearts without restraint can make us feel vulnerable, which is something we typically avoid. Most of us have to relearn the skill of imaginative, emotionally engaged play. This practice can help.

PRACTICE

This is not an intellectual exercise—it's a writing strategy that embraces curiosity and love, to help you create characters that feel truly alive on the page.

Start with your curiosity. Get to know your characters by asking them questions, just like you do with the real people in your life. Run this Q&A in your bullet journal. Ask them questions in your own voice, and when you write their responses, allow their voice, personality, and perspective to come through in their words.

Here are some examples of questions you could ask: What do you like to eat for breakfast? How did you learn how to shave? What do you want out of life? Why do you curl your hair the way you do? What book is on your bedside table? What was your most embarrassing moment? Why did you pick a fight with your brother? What did it feel like to kiss your best friend's wife?

You can ask your characters anything you want. There are no limits. Explore, ask more questions, and meander through their stories and memories. Dig deep, and be brave and unreasonable when you ask them about who they are.

Note: You don't need to know every single thing about your character before you let them show up in the story you're writing. As long as you're curious or fascinated by the details you do know, that's enough to start. Remember that they are their own person, and they can forget to tell you things—or keep things from you on purpose. Allow them to surprise you while you're writing them in a scene. Sometimes these surprises are plot twists, and those become the best part of the story.

Once you've explored your character's inner life and you've learned some interesting details about who they are, you're ready to make them come alive with the power of make-believe. Now is the time to practise suspending your disbelief to bridge the gap between imagination and reality. You do this by pretending your character is real, in the same way pretending made Sock real.

To do this, write your character a note as if they were a real person. Address them by name and let them know that you're going to write about them. If there's a specific scene you want to explore, let them know what it is—perhaps an event from their past or a decision they're facing in your story.

Ask your character for help as you write them. Be explicit: ask them to give you the right words.

Now open your freewriting notebook. Spend ten to fifteen minutes writing a scene with this character, allowing yourself to fully believe in their reality as you write. Let the character's presence guide your writing.

THE POWER OF A COLLECTIVE

Before I published my first book, I received an invitation to join a collective called the Toronto Writers Salon. It wasn't exactly a secret society, but it was exclusive, and I felt lucky to be invited. As part of the Salon, seasoned authors (famous ones!) hung out with emerging writers like me.

We took turns hosting events; these were fancy cocktail parties, potlucks, and backyard hot tub parties. We met to discuss special topics, like how running is like writing, how to organize a plot, and who the good agents are.

From this community, I learned the business and craft of writing, much more quickly than I could have alone. It was so valuable to be in conversation with other writers: the whisper-network education, editorial advice, and deep, difficult, delicious talks about money, power, and psychology were enlightening. When I heard published authors confess to feeling stuck on a story problem or hurt by a bad review, I thought, *If that's how they feel, maybe I am a real writer!*

As individual writers, we worked in different fields and wrote from a variety of perspectives. Our written themes, stories, and genres overlapped and diverged. The one thing that connected us was our love of writing. And this connection was enough to keep us united.

Ideas and stories move freely through time and space. As writers, thinkers, and storytellers, it's in our nature to motivate each other through creative abundance and interdependence. The books we read now will become part of our unconscious map of the world. The books we write now might become the seeds of future books—both our own and those written by other writers.

A good writing collective is made up of writers who understand that ideas and stories are ever-evolving and infinite, and that books are stronger and more interesting when they pay attention to each other. Writers in a secure collective fill their cups when they talk to each other about what they're doing. They amplify their creative energy by writing together.

Connection fuels innovation; ideas create more ideas. The social economy of our writing life is abundant: our resources multiply when shared, and this is how our collective consciousness expands. Imaginative intelligence is limitless.

By contrast, the traditional publishing economy is built on scarcity. It's competitive: every season, out of the hundreds of books they publish, each major publisher tries to make one the "winner" so it will sell lots and lots of copies. The industry keeps a lot of important parts of the business a secret, like who has the most well-connected publicists, the going rates for advances, which books get extra money to help them be blockbusters, or which books get submitted for big cash prizes. Which means that as publishers compete in the market, writers are pitted against each other.

All of this can be alienating for authors, who need to work together to feel secure and creatively tapped in.

Writing collectives exist because they maintain the strength of this connection between writers. You're not alone: you and your writing are already part of this network. If you don't feel that way, join a writing group, or start one.

PRACTICE

You can start your collective with just one or two writers you've met in a workshop, or at an open mic or book launch, or through social media. You can meet in person or virtually, or a combination of the two. Your group doesn't need to include published authors, but it should include writers who are supportive and non-competitive. Make an agreement with each other: promise to speak to each other with integrity and honesty, to protect each other's creative curiosity, to share any helpful resources and information you may have, and to celebrate each other's successes. Allow yourself to tap into connection and to write from that amplified source of energy.

*

HOW TO WRITE AN ENDING

As you get closer to the end of your draft, the writing might feel more difficult. Writing a story typically involves three distinct phases, each with its own challenges and rewards:

1. Writing the first part of a story requires active curiosity: it's about set-up, exploration, and development. This part contains the essence of intrigue.

2. Writing the middle part of a story requires bravery: it's about designing tough situations for your characters. This part contains the essence of challenge.

3. Writing the final part of a story requires surrender: it's about resolving conflicts and bringing the narrative to a satisfying conclusion. This part contains the essence of transformation.

In the beginning, you're buoyed by the natural momentum that accompanies your creative discovery. This is like preparing for a party: you're chilling the champagne, arranging the flowers, and hanging up twinkly lights.

During the middle stage, you're like a tightrope walker balanced between uncertainty and faith. You don't know how your characters are going to overcome the obstacles they face, but you have an invisible safety net: you trust that your process will guide you. You keep writing because you understand that you won't know the full story until you finish writing it.

As you approach the final stage and move toward the ending, a new set of challenges emerges. This is where the difficulty often intensifies, and where many writers struggle to bring their story to a close.

If your story is about change or transformation—if it includes an arc that resolves through some combination of intrigue, challenge, and surrender—you'll have to embody and manifest the essences of intrigue, challenge, and surrender as you write.

Writing the last part of your story requires you to embrace the essence of surrender: the release that precedes insight.

If you've set the stakes high for your character, the resolution to your story likely won't be easy and straightforward. And writing the ending probably won't be easy for you either. If you feel afraid to face your final scenes, or frustrated because you keep trying and failing to harmonize all of your story's elements, you've tapped into precisely the energy you'll need to release and transform into surrender in order to write your ending.

To do this, feel your difficult feelings and keep writing anyway. As you approach the end of your book, take note of your own physiology and neurochemistry. Literally write them down in your notebook. *I'm wired and tired. My body buzzes with energy and won't settle. My neck feels stiff. My clothes feel too tight.*

You can share this energy with your character—there's a good chance you can use it to express something on their behalf. As you wrestle with completion, you can also allow the emotions you're experiencing to infuse your descriptions. This gives you presence. *Detective Bertel had another sleepless night, waking frantically at 3:00 a.m., haunted by a dream about the unsolved murder case. She holds her body stiffly and avoids turning her head to answer her partner's questions. Her breathing is shallow, and her blazer is tight around her shoulders, constricting her movements. Despite her discomfort, she feels compelled to fulfill the role she has chosen. She knows she must make the call that will forever change someone's life.*

You'll likely be fully present in the final scene as you're writing it, which means you might not know you're writing your ending until you finish the last word of your final sentence.

Presence is being in the moment. Write from within that moment. If you feel like it's just too hard, this is a good sign that you're working with dramatic tension. Resisting this tension will feel like suffering. Instead, acknowledge it and bring it into your scenes so that dramatic tension can help propel your story to its end.

The feeling that precedes surrender isn't a problem you need to solve. Instead, let it be an arrow that guides you home.

*

FINISH WHAT YOU START

A story is not real life, but it can be a powerful symbol for life. If you've infused your story with your presence, energy, and attention, it's likely that your state of mind has become the book's consciousness. As you approach the end of your story, it's time to set boundaries that will separate you from what you've created. It's time to finish writing your book and then move on to the next phase of your life.

Like beginnings, endings can feel scary, too. You're leaving a comfort zone and heading into unknown territory.

On the other side of finishing your book lies the daunting question "What's next?" Yikes. Of course, you can't actually know what's next—new opportunities and ideas might arise that you can't even imagine at this point.

Your filters of seeing, knowing, and understanding will change after you finish your current project. After resolving your story's dilemmas or conflicts, you'll understand something new about the human condition. You'll probably see the world a little differently.

"What's next?" is an alarming question.

Are you continuing to work on your book so you don't have to face that question? There is a price to not finishing your work. You may experience a dull ache—your growth is suppressed. It may also present as an agitation, a constantly spinning hum that comes from holding yourself back. Release that energy and let it carry you to the finish line.

Finishing feels different than flow. Paddling a canoe down a river takes focus and energy, but slowing the canoe as you paddle to the riverbank takes strength and power and precision, because the river continues to move you forward as you try to slow down.

Finishing is a decision you make. All stories can keep going, of course, if we choose to let them. Which means finishing is an arbitrary decision you get to make as an artist.

Final energy is brave. It's curious, too. It's attuned to the act of stopping, to the way people say no, to the finality of locks clicking shut and gates swinging closed. For me, this energy manifests in a heightened awareness of physical textures and finishes. I notice smooth or rough surfaces, transparency and opacity, the sheen of lacquer or the understated elegance of matte.

This might seem unconventional, but as a kinesthetic learner, I process abstract concepts through tangible, sensory experiences. Just as I choose ink colours to match the emotional tone of my writing, I use these physical observations to understand and embody the essence of completion.

Completion is fascinated by cessation: a bicycle wheel gradually slowing to a stop, a spinning top wobbling before it tips into stillness, the various ways songs conclude, from the jarring energy of a guitar chord to a slow, gentle fade-out. Completion sees itself in the clean lines of empty seed pods, the stark simplicity of animal bones, the finality of a signature on a contract.

The beginning and middle stages of your project explore the energy of infinite possibilities, whereas the energy of completion embraces the limits of what is possible. Your ending gets to be whatever you want it to be, so embody the consciousness of completion. Use your creative curiosity to decide when to end your book, just to see what it would feel like. You know your manuscript is finished because you decide to end it.

To end a project, adjust your focus. Pay attention to the conclusions, resolutions, and limits that surround you—both in your writing and in your physical environment. Embody the energy of completion in order to understand how it feels. This next practice is designed to help you know when to make a full stop.

PRACTICE

Write down your observations of completion in your bullet journal. Other questions to consider in your journalling: How can the energy of completion you've observed help you make decisions about ending your book? What would it feel like to embrace the limits of what's possible in your story?

*

THE MIXOLOGY OF COMPLETION

Get used to finishing things in real life to learn how it feels to finish your book. Start with the annoying slivers of soap left in your shower: use them up or throw them out, and start fresh with a new bar of soap. Do you have almost-finished jars of mustard, pickles, and hot sauce in your fridge? Finish them off and recycle the jars. The same goes for those almost-finished books you're reading, magazines you're halfway through, and the podcast series you started but didn't complete. Make time to finish them, or decide to not finish them to clear the space they're taking up on your shelves and in your brain.

As you complete the uncompleted things around you, or as you let them go, notice that each time you check something off your list—whether it is a task you were dreading or a pleasure you were looking forward to—you have made a *choice*. Enjoy the power you wield! Get to know the crisp feeling of making a permanent mark on your environment and the feeling of clarity that comes from it. You're a person who finishes things!

Completion is a creative choice, which means it's also a good time to use your curiosity. That's why closure feels so expansive, fun, and spacious. Look at the clear space in your fridge, your fresh soap dish, the neater rows on your bookshelves. Appreciate your choice to end things as a way to make room for more possibility in your life.

Now bring this state of mind to finishing your book.

Keep in mind that ending a book is like catching a Frisbee: it requires you to be decisive and go with the flow at the same time. The ecosystem of your story changes moment to moment, so while it's true that you get to decide when and where your piece of writing will end, you've also got to remain flexible and open to surprise twists. The following practice will help you do this.

PRACTICE

1. Know your personal sensations of creative completion. Choose something in your physical surroundings to finish. Keep the stakes low: that last teaspoon of soy sauce at the bottom of the bottle. (Bonus points for choosing something you've been avoiding for a while!) Decide that you'll repair, discard, donate, delegate, or otherwise finish this thing. As you take action, pay attention to how your body feels before, during, and after you finish it. Write in your bullet journal about your feelings, as if you were a scientist observing an experiment in a petri dish. For example:

   • Before I return this unread library book, my chest feels prickly and edgy.

- While I am actively sliding the book through the return slot, my chest feels calm and curious.

- After I return it, my chest feels light and clear. I also feel a bit hungry.

Do this a few times with different physical tasks until you begin to recognize your personal internal somatic patterns. Once you have a sense of your signature completion sensations in your body and your mind, go to the next step.

2. Connect these sensations to your writing process. As you write, watch for the arrival of the sensations you observed in the first step above. For example, pay attention when that prickly, edgy feeling appears, or when you notice that calm and curious feeling in your chest. These are signs that you're likely approaching a stage of completion or breakthrough in your writing. Your brain is a reliable mixologist, and it concocts intricate recipes of neurochemicals that influence your thoughts, emotions, and physical sensations. In this case, these sensations let you know that a specific neurochemical blend associated with *I'm going to finish something* has been released into your neural pathways. When you know this signature sensation of completion in your body, and know the sensations that precede it, you'll better recognize when you're close to finishing something.

3. Let the intelligence of your body lead you to your story's ending. Notice all the other subtle ways your body tells you what it wants you to know. These may include your breathing (shallow or deep, jagged or steady), your hand-

writing (loose and relaxed, smaller or larger than usual). Read the negative space, too: some of your body's signals might be in the form of what's not there (think about any chronic conditions you may have, like allergies, pain, or nervous habits—whether your body is more at ease or more inflamed). These all carry important information for you. Attune yourself to these messages and follow their lead.

A hint: You can trust that you're in the energy of integration and resolution when you feel a sense of peace in your body. You may feel agitated, tense, or activated as you approach your story's conclusion—this might feel like the slow upward climb of a roller coaster before it speeds down the track. The act of finishing, though, is ultimately one of acceptance. You can actually feel quite serene once you get to the end, even if you're writing about an epic battle or a scene where your protagonist surrenders to her deepest fear.

Your ending might not come the way you expect, but as long as you follow your internal signs toward that feeling of completion, you'll know when you've arrived.

AFTER THE BOOK IS WRITTEN

Once you've finished your manuscript, give yourself some time to wrap things up. Take time to reflect on the experience. And before you dive into your next project, rest. Do nothing for a bit. Let yourself settle into your new identity as a writer who has finished writing a book.

I know it's tempting to keep the momentum going. But your thoughts have been so focused on one project for so long that they've patterned themselves to work in a certain way. It's time to let those patterns go. Reflection, celebration, and rest give your mind the time it needs to digest and metabolize what you've learned from writing this book. Most of this happens behind the scenes while you sleep through an unconscious settling and rearranging of neurology.

You're no longer someone who wants to write; you're someone who has written. You've entered a new timeline.

If writing a book was a big dream of yours, you've just met one of your life's goals. If you didn't believe you were capable of writing a full book, you've just changed your reality. If you're a lawyer or a teacher or an athlete—you've just changed your identity. Soon, you might want to write something new: another story, project, or creation. But first, it's important to pause and to let any changes fully alchemize.

Later, after you've taken time to reflect and digest, it's time to acknowledge and celebrate. Congratulations are in order! Share your news, sip pink champagne, hold a finishing party, or go into the woods and arrange some acorns in concentric circles—whatever marks the moment as special for you. The following practice is designed to help you wrap things up with internal reflection.

PRACTICE

Give yourself a day or two to reflect on the questions below. Don't rush your answers. Linger on what you've learned, what worked for you, and what's most important to you about your writing process. This lets your unconscious mind know what you want to take from this whole experience, how you've changed, and what you want it to remember the next time you create something new. Think of this practice as installing a software upgrade: it may take a bit of time, but things will work more smoothly and efficiently after the upgrade is complete. Once this learning settles into your unconscious, it becomes your lived wisdom.

Put on music that soothes you into a creative trance, and set a timer for thirty minutes each time you sit down to answer these questions in your bullet journal:

- What worked for you in the process of writing this book?

- What do you want to remember?

- When you were stuck, how did you move through that impasse?

- What advice would you give your past self, knowing what you know now?

- What reliably inspires you?

- What did your writing know all along that you needed to learn?

- What conditions are best for your creative curiosity?

- What do you want more of?

- What are you ready to stop doing?

- Who are you as a writer now?

- What do you appreciate about the process of writing?

*

YOUR STORY IS SMARTER
THAN YOU ARE

One of the most exciting things about writing a book is that you might only understand your whole book after you've written it. When you write with creative curiosity, you're in a flow state and tapping into your unconscious mind. Which means your first draft holds all sorts of significance you might not be aware of yet. You might not even remember whole elaborate chunks of the story you wrote.

Block off time to read your first draft with an open mind. No interruptions. No corrections, editing, or judgment. This is the single most important thing you'll do before you start your second draft: make space for your own neutrality and curiosity and get to know the entity you've written. Give yourself a weekend away with your manuscript if you can.

What does your story know that you don't? Approach your draft with curiosity. Look for the elements that fascinate you the most and make note of all the passages where you forget that you're reading something you wrote. Allow yourself to be surprised What's your story trying to show you?

In a second draft, you're going to follow clues you've set out, pick up bread crumbs, and map out the story. You won't necessarily start on page one, tinkering and tightening every line until you reach the end. To make the story clear, you're probably going to have to write chunks of new information, new characters, and new structures. You might even experiment with the sound of your voice and style.

A story becomes a truer version of itself through polishing and refurbishing, improving a word choice here and an image there, and most of all by being genuinely open to the essential or deeper meaning of the story. This is going to take time, energy, and curiosity. You're going to be fascinated as you go, because now you get to work with a creation that has its own inherent wisdom—one that's likely to surprise you with insights and connections you didn't consciously craft. The unconscious intelligence within your story often reveals itself in ways that feel smarter or more cohesive than you might have intentionally planned. This can make the revision process feel illuminating and revelatory at times.

In your second draft, you'll probably get to know your story's authentic spirit (if you haven't already); revising is like collaborating with a strong creative partner that knows what it values. Once you understand what it is your story wants you to know, your revisions should become easier. As you concentrate on integrating all the elements of your story—the plot, characters, themes, and newly discovered insights—stay open to that deep sense of enjoyment that comes with being in flow. Focus and flexibility will keep you right on the edge of where challenge meets skill.

*

SHOWING YOUR CREATION

As you approach the completion of your first draft, you'll likely consider sharing it with someone else. You're actually going to let them read it. Consciously, this is what you want: it's what you're here for. But unconsciously, your mind is aware that sharing your work will change everything. Change brings the unknown, and the unknown is potentially dangerous.

You gave yourself permission to write without knowing if what you wrote would be good. You boldly set boundaries around your time, practised your craft consistently, and travelled beyond the edges of your comfort zone to fulfill your personal desire to write. You learned how to put yourself in a light trance to enhance your curiosity and creativity, and how to let your intuition guide you. You adapted to write through so much uncertainty, and you did all of this work in solitude. What will other people think when they see what you've done?

You may have written your book to fulfill a personal need, but showing your creation is an opportunity for another kind of transformation—think of the way blue and yellow exist as separate colours yet combine to make the colour green. Unconsciously, your mind is afraid of what might happen when you mix your comfort zone (blue) with a new element (yellow). Once you've done this, you can't undo it. There are real consequences when you share your story. Showing your manuscript to someone else means an as yet unseen part of yourself will be seen.

Sharing your writing opens you up to connection and belonging, as well as criticism and judgment. It can lead to personal growth, new opportunities, and a deeper understanding of yourself. It's valid to be hesitant about showing your work to someone else. It takes courage!

Choose your first reader with care. Ideally, this is someone who understands the vulnerable nature of a first draft: a fellow writer, a trusted friend with literary sensibilities, or a writing group member who appreciates the creative process. You want to invite someone who understands how to handle a sprout with an underdeveloped root system. At this stage, your work isn't meant to be polished or publication-ready. The goal is to receive encouraging and constructive feedback that nurtures your creative spirit and guides you toward strengthening your story. Your first reader should understand that delicate balance.

Writing isn't just about words—it's about emotion, energy, and life. Positive feedback lets you know that you've made a successful transmission. In a first draft, it doesn't matter if it's "good"—only that it contains energy. Words are how we direct this energy. What's working? Where is the reader most engaged? What are their strongest emotional experiences?

Where do the details sparkle? It's important to follow that energy as you're writing, as these points of energy will guide you during revisions. External feedback can help you see that energy.

A good first reader respects creative energy when they encounter it. They know how to honour and appreciate creative work at every stage, because the terrain first drafts typically cover is often confusing and uneven, with weird looping trails and dead-end streets where the narrative spins out until it stalls. (To be clear, these things are totally normal.)

If the thought of sharing your work gives you sweaty palms, sugar cravings, shortness of breath, or puts you in a super-distracted mode, congratulations—you care about what you've written. That's why it feels like something is at stake. This is actually a good thing! Close your eyes and picture your writing being received with curiosity, love, and care. What does it feel like when you receive that kind of response? Hang out with the feelings this stirs up for you. Let your feelings settle in and send a message to your inner protector: this is how you want it to feel when you share your work.

Whenever you feel nervous before showing your writing, recall those positive feelings. It will settle your nervous system and alleviate the fear responses of fight, flight, or freeze.

Try to appreciate your creative work in all of its stages. Trust that your writing can withstand someone else's eyes and opinions. Your book wants to be read. This is also why you wrote it. You and your writing are both stronger than you think.

When to share your work

At what point in your writing process should you share a first draft or second draft? The best time is often when you've reached a plateau in your growth with the piece—when you're starting to feel slightly disconnected from it (perhaps even a bit bored). Try to resist sharing your work when you're frustrated or truly stuck on a story problem (though asking for specific advice in those moments can be helpful). Give yourself the incredible benefits of wrestling with your dilemma first.

There's plenty of research in cognitive psychology and education that proves that we learn best when we have to work through vexing problems without being given an easy answer. The term for this is *productive struggle*. It's also been shown that we get way better outcomes when we see challenges as opportunities for growth. This is known as *growth mindset*. Whatever you want to call this skill-building kind of puzzle-solving, try to wait until you feel you've genuinely taken your piece as far as you can on your own before you share it and ask for feedback.

At that point, give it a break from your attention for a couple of weeks. When you come back to it, look at your writing with curiosity and an open mind to see if you're still actively engaged in productive struggle. You'll know you've taken it as far as you can when you still feel vaguely interested in it, but the electric charge of energy has gone.

Imagine looking down at your work from the upper floors of a tall building—you're no longer on the same level as the writing, but observing it from a distance. This perspective shift often happens after you've completed a first or second draft and have let it rest for a while.

You'll know you're ready to share your work when the questions that initially challenged you about the piece no longer feel as pressing or exciting. At this point, sharing your work and receiving feedback will introduce a new level of challenge, require you to engage different skills, and see your writing through fresh eyes.

This slight detachment doesn't mean you no longer care about your work. It simply shows that you've reached a natural pause in your individual journey with the piece. This is the perfect time to invite others into the process.

PRACTICE

These guidelines can help you feel grounded before you send your work to a reader. They will also ensure that you and your reader understand each other, which should make for a successful collaboration.

1. Before you send anyone your work, ask for their permission. Let them know the length of your document and set a realistic time frame for them to read it and get back to you.

2. Tell them what kind of feedback you want. Be generous with your honesty and specificity. For example, do you want witnessing and reflection? Do you want creative idea-sharing and discussion? Do you have specific questions about an element of craft or story structure? You can also ask your reader to provide feedback to you spe-

cifically in the form of appreciations, questions, and/or suggestions.

3. If it's a long piece, consider highlighting specific sections you want feedback on.

4. Don't apologize for your writing in any way before sending it. Do let your reader know it's a first draft. (This is not an apology; it shows awareness of your creative process.) A sentence or two of context is fine, but resist explaining any meaning, influences, or anything else that could get in the way of your reader's fresh experience of the writing.

5. Prepare yourself mentally and emotionally for receiving feedback by practising self-compassion as your reader is reviewing your work. Reflect on your accomplishments, write and listen to positive affirmations, and treat yourself with extra kindness and respect during this time.

*

YOUR WRITING HOLDS POWER

Your writing is not a static object. It's full of energy.

A story becomes real because of who you are when you're writing it. You breathe life into it with your care and attention. That's what makes it feel alive.

When you write with presence, your writing remains vivid and authentic, regardless of how much time has passed since you wrote it.

You can jot down a note today about the way the sun shines into your glass of ice water and casts a golden glow on the table, even though you might not find a place for that detail in your writing for years.

But writing holds power, like a battery. It will last. You might not know what you're going to power with that detail, so your job is to hold on to it until you need it.

An idea you wanted to write a whole story about last year

could turn into character development for the novel you're going to write next year.

Your writing doesn't have an expiration date. Those pages of handwriting in your notebook don't care what day, month, or year it is. You can always go back to your old notes to find batteries when you need them. Personally, I don't even date my old freewriting notebooks; I have no sequential system to keep them in order. That's because when I go back for inspiration, I'm not usually looking for a specific time or date—I'm looking for energy.

When you need new material or a spark of inspiration, flip through your old notebooks randomly to see what jumps out at you. Highlight a few words and phrases that have sparkle or mystery, and copy them into your current notebook. The act of copying can recharge them for you to use to write something new.

Writing time is non-linear. Writing with presence, your work can transcend time. Your words capture the essence of the present moment, draw from your past experiences and emotions, and hold value and meaning for future readers. When you're writing in a whole-minded state, you do this all at once without even thinking about it. And once you're aware that your writing is timeless, you can use this to your advantage.

Waiting for news about the acceptance of a piece for publication can take a very long time. Let's say you wait for eight months, and then one of your stories comes back with a rejection letter. It can be tempting to look backwards and think: *If I had worked harder on this story last year before I submitted it, I could have published it by now!* We live most of our lives in linear time, and the habit of thinking about your work in linear time is deeply ingrained, thanks to cultural and societal structures that reward productivity by the clock.

Take a deep breath whenever you need to come back to the present moment. What if the value of your story existed outside of time? Could you look at it differently?

It's been eight months, and your life has changed since you sent out this piece for consideration. You've learned a few things, and this has made you a different writer. You're working on something else now. It's hard to remember what you were trying to do when you wrote that older story—and it doesn't matter anyway. What should you do with it now?

Feeling alienated from your old writing is normal. Your ideas and identity keep evolving, so an old story might not reflect your present obsessions and concerns and tastes. Hang out with it anyway for a minute to receive the gifts it might have to offer.

Your old story can tell you something about who and where you are at this very moment if you try to connect to it with presence. You have grown since you last wrote those words, so as you reread them, look ahead to new possibilities with curiosity and respect for the writer you used to be.

When you revisit your writing after time away from it, ask yourself: *Where can I find presence in this writing now? Where is the energy, and how can I work with that energy today?*

The best possible editor for an older story is the writer you are right now—especially if you're returning to edits eight months post-submission. And your story is smart. You can ask it for clues. Look for glimmers and sparkles of interest as you read it. What you notice about your old writing will tell you what you need to write next.

Follow the energy. Focus on the parts of your old stories and drafts that feel the most alive, and start writing and revising from there.

*

REVISION IS EVOLUTION

All the writers we truly admire demonstrate a blend of humility and audacity. You understand this paradox—as a writer, you live it, too.

You have to be humble enough to pay attention, see the truth in a scene, and write it down honestly. You write your story even though you don't necessarily know what it all really means. You surrender. You write to the end, even though you have a sinking feeling that the shimmering beauty of your idea is becoming more ramshackle as you attempt to get it down.

You feel compelled to finish your story anyway, so you do.

You show your work to a trusted reader for feedback. They're honest, and you humbly listen to them. Ugh, how could you not have seen all the holes in your story? It's so obvious to you now.

So you work on your revision and try to "fix" everything that's "wrong" with the story.

You do your best. You rewrite until you don't recognize your own words anymore. You feel emptied out. On one hand, you feel clear, clean, because there's nothing left unwritten inside you. But on the other hand, you're completely confused. Where does the story end and where do you begin? Your edges are blurry. You want to sleep or laugh or cry. You've done everything you can to the story at this point (you think). You're done.

So what do you do next? You dare to put your story out more widely so somebody else can read it. You don't know if it's any good or not, but you send it out anyway. Talk about humility and audacity. That takes nerve.

Think about a book or a story you love. See if you can connect to the author's boldness. They *wrote* that. Can you feel the energy of their daring? Can you feel how they've let go of the trapeze bar in order to release their story to you?

Now see if you can connect to their unsureness. They wrote *that*. Can you feel how they've tried to achieve a result on a scale that has no number? Can you feel that, no matter how hard they try, they will never really know if their best is good enough, or if they stuck their landing?

Your story is alive. Revising your creative writing is not like taking your car to a mechanic for a repair. The nature of mechanical repairs is corrective in that it's focused on fixing specific problems. The nature of revision is generative—it's a journey of growth and discovery. Revisions are where you get to explore new ideas, tend deeper insights, and learn what your story is really trying to share with others—and what it's asking from you.

If you adjust the way you perceive revisions, then the problem of "fixing" your first draft disappears. The purpose of your work becomes clear: you're tending a living thing and helping it come into a more mature and developed form of itself. You're a patient, creative gardener. A compassionate puppy trainer. An attentive and wise grandparent.

When you show up to revise your draft with a balance of humility and daring—poised on the knife's edge between the known and unknown—your work can bring you into a new paradigm of thought that understands your story is nuanced and expressive and ultimately subjective.

Is it good or bad? is an unhelpful question. *What is it for?* is a better one.

Revising your work will reveal your creative edges and push you toward your next level of awareness. Riding your own edge is sensitive and mysterious work. It requires courage and resilience. But it's worth it—the alternative is inertia and stagnation.

This practice prepares you for revisions by having you reflect on your intentions. The goal is to shift your mindset toward growth and discovery instead of fixing what's "broken."

PRACTICE

Before you start revising your work in progress, ask yourself a few of the questions listed below. Write your responses freely in your bullet journal, without editing or rereading, for five to ten minutes, until you feel your body relax and settle. You may not get a satisfying answer to any of these questions in your freewriting, but that doesn't matter. The revised version of your story, which you're about to write, will be the real answer.

What am I writing for?

What does my story want?

How does my story want to be written?

What does my story have in store for me?

What does my story want to show me?

Who do I have to be in order to revise this story?

What have I left unsaid that wants to be said?

The goal of freewriting in response to these questions is to prepare you for revision by activating and focusing your curiosity and guiding it to revise your story in meaningful ways.

*

BREAK IT LIKE A GEODE

Revising is daunting because there's a sense of calcification and finality that encloses a piece of writing once it's been transcribed into type. This feeling can grow even more pronounced once those typed pages are printed. It feels so good to see printed pages, though, doesn't it? Printing makes your writing feel real.

A printed first draft looks exactly like a printed final draft. It's the same ink, the same font, the same line spacing. Your printed pages can convince you that an early draft of your manuscript is rock-solid, polished, done. But it isn't rock-solid. It's a draft. And your next job with a first draft is to break it, like a geode, to find the sparkling crystals within.

Smash your story open before you start revising it. Discover what's most alive and relevant about the beautiful, exciting story living inside the black-and-white shell of your text. If you work from a new document, your draft is still saved on your computer, so the stakes are actually low—revisions and edits don't have to be final. The next exercise will help you give yourself permission to start changing what you've already written.

PRACTICE

This exercise is a good one to try after you've finished your first draft but before you start revising. It's especially useful for pieces of writing you haven't looked at for a while or when you want to move forward but don't quite know how to proceed.

Cut up your printed pages, literally, with scissors. Mix the chapters and elements around on the floor or spread them out on a big table. Get physical: move your sentences and pages around with your hands, mark them up with highlighters and coloured pencils, and let your whole body get involved in this restructuring adventure. This is big-picture editing. It's not the time to be tidy.

When you see your different characters and timelines shuffled around, scenes from the beginning touching scenes from the end, you'll likely spot all kinds of insights and patterns that were hidden in your story. Get these into your bullet journal so you remember what you're learning as you mix everything up.

When you bend down to peer at your words in the mess of pages, you'll probably also notice the idiosyncrasies of your own language: your most-used words, echoed phrases, and images. You'll see how much dialogue you've written versus passages of descriptive prose.

Pay attention to anything you want to try, change, enhance, add, or delete in your next draft. Record these observations as a set of instructions you can follow. For example, *Add more subtext to the dialogue in the party scene* or *Write the flashbacks in present tense.* Take the time to write them down—if certain changes need to be done in a specific order, prioritize them accordingly. For everything else, a list of bullet points is fine.

You can now recycle your cut-up pieces of paper. Clean up your work area. You have your instructions and to-do list. Now you can bring your insights back to the version that you've saved on your computer and get to work.

*

HERE BE MONSTERS

Some writers are adept at compartmentalizing their fear and doubt, and can push their inner protector aside to write their first draft quickly. They can plug their ears and sing "la la la la la" so they don't hear those internal warnings. While this approach can work for some, it's not a method I advocate or use personally.

In my experience, truly engaging with our creative process means acknowledging and working with our inner protector, not ignoring it.

When it's time to read your first draft, you'll likely find that every creative decision you made while ignoring the protests of your inner protector is a jump scare. Your pages are laced with hidden monsters—they're lurking in your sentences. Once you're courageous enough to read your own pages, you may encounter the worst version of your inner critic's voice offering heavy judgments like *This is clearly the worst thing ever written.* Or your inner protector will spring into action with warnings: *Stop! Danger! Don't go any further!*

How can you approach revision when it's so emotionally treacherous?

If you're trying to start work on a second draft and these voices sound familiar, know that this is totally normal. Your nervous system is likely in freeze, fight, or flight mode, and this is an opportunity for you to make friends with your inner protector (and your inner critic) and learn how to read your work in progress with creative curiosity.

Before arming yourself with a red pencil and highlighter and diving back into your first draft with changes, give yourself grace. Approach your discomfort with care and wonder. The places in your manuscript that feel scary aren't actually monsters. They're spots where you may have pushed beyond your comfort zone without fully realizing it, with the permission of your inner protector, in your disciplined race to finish the first draft. Now's the time to bring in your curiosity. How can you meet these new edges of growth?

Work with your body to relieve your stress and clear adrenaline. Easy ways to do this include inhaling and exhaling deeply (big sighs are very good), with or without counting the number of breaths you take, shaking and dancing, having a cry, singing along to a song or playlist you love.

If, after trying the above, you're still seeing monsters in your first draft, call a writing friend and ask them to sit with you (virtually or in person) as you quietly read some of your own work. It's surprisingly easier to read your own pages when you have someone supportive by your side.

*

TRUST YOUR CRAFT

I once lost a file of a finished, polished story. I hadn't printed a hard copy. The file contained the best version of a story I'd written and revised multiple times over four years. I was at the Banff Centre for Arts and Creativity, using a borrowed hard drive to back up my work, and the file became corrupted. Unreadable. I was supposed to submit the final draft of this story to my mentor the next day, but the story was gone. I was devastated. I cried hot tears of frustration and hopelessness and I barely resisted the urge to throw the treacherous hard drive across the room. The thought of losing four years of work was almost unbearable. But I had no choice—I had to rewrite it from scratch. From memory. In twenty-four hours.

I did it. I didn't have time to write self-consciously—I just wrote it all down as fast as I could type, relying on body memory as much as anything else. And I submitted it on time the next day. My new version of that story was far superior to the version I lost. It's impossible to prove this, of course, but I know it's true.

I didn't have to start from scratch, really: I had grown along with my revisions. I couldn't go back to that lost version if I tried, because my writing skills had improved. The new speed-written version of my story contained all the years of improvements, but it was written in one solid voice instead of a patchwork of edits.

This experience taught me how to recognize what a true revision looks like.

Your first draft was written by an earlier version of yourself. As time moves forward, you collect more skills, more knowledge, and more experience. You can't unknow what you know. And it's not just conscious knowledge floating around as thoughts in your head—you've also gained unconscious knowledge and insight.

I had written all of my versions of that story with my whole mind. Writing with your whole mind means as you create scenes for your story, your brain stores them in a way similar to how it stores actual experiences. It's saving the essence of these scenes, not cluttering your consciousness with every word, but codifying them as vivid, accessible memories. You can retrieve these scenes whenever you need them, not necessarily word for word, but in a more efficient, harmonized form. Trust that they're there; they were for me.

When you begin to rewrite your book, remember that your story exists beyond the page. The page is just a marker, like a sign posted on a hiking trail that shows you how the trail is organized. Looking at the sign is a different experience than walking along the trail. You're writing a book to transmit the energy and experience of a story to your readers. You may do this through pages and words, but language is not the same as story.

Knowing this, you can release your grip on your story's current page-based shape. You can bring it back into form more easily a second time, because your story already knows how to live on the page.

To understand how this works, try to write your second draft from scratch. Even if you have written a long, intricately plotted novel, you can still use this practice: you just need to consult your outline, if you have one, and break the practice into smaller chunks first by rewriting it chapter by chapter. If you don't have an outline for your novel, use this practice to try to write an outline from scratch.

This exercise will help you tap into the deeper, internalized knowledge you've gained about your story and characters, allowing you to recreate and improve upon your work with fresh eyes and current skills.

PRACTICE

While there are many ways to approach revision, including non-linear methods that allow you to playfully explore your story's deeper themes and connections, sometimes a fresh, linear rewrite is the most effective and enjoyable way to go.

This exercise will teach you how it feels to let go of your first draft and revise freely, as you rely on your internalized knowledge about your story and characters. It might seem labour-intensive at first, but trust me: the return on your investment makes this practice well worth your time. Do it once and you're likely to feel more confident about how many details you remember. Then, tune into this mindset whenever you want to reconnect to the "unlanguaged" source of your story.

This can also be a great technique to use when you feel boxed in and uninspired by something you've already written. For example, you can try rewriting your story's beginning or ending from scratch, just to get a new perspective.

Open a new document on your computer. You'll use this to compose your second draft. You don't have to rely on your memory to rewrite it. Just keep a hard copy of your first draft beside you as you write your second draft so you can consult it as you go. If there are any major changes you want to make to your outline, work those out on paper before you start your second draft. Put your revised outline up where you can see it and write your second draft according to the new plan.

Start writing from scene one. You're going to write your revision with the same open, exploratory spirit you used for your first draft, but it's going to feel much more focused this time because now you know so much more about your characters and your story. When you need to re-envision and re-embody your previously written scenes, you can access the memories of them by returning to your whole-minded state.

A reliable way for me to do this is to engage in focused freewriting. For instance, I might spend five minutes writing without stopping about a specific character or setting, allowing my mind to reconnect with the vivid details and emotions of that scene. This targeted freewriting helps me tap into the essence of what I've previously created, making it easier to bring those scenes back to life in my revision.

As you rewrite each scene, steal glances at your hard copy. Doing so will keep you oriented and inspired. Look ahead to your new outline for direction. Most importantly, follow the energy you feel in the current of your rewriting.

You are the conduit for your story. You know how to write it because you've done it before. Your second draft will be much easier to write when you let go of your first draft. You've got this.

*

BREAK YOUR OWN SPELL

In your second draft, it can feel immensely satisfying to make the embroidered edge of the tablecloth "turquoise" instead of "light blue." But if you're going to cut the whole farmhouse kitchen scene out of your story later, the colour of that thread doesn't matter. It's a better use of your time to get the core pieces of your story in place before you start on smaller edits.

Your second or third draft is typically where you focus on big-picture elements: you solidify your story's structure, characters, plot points, and overarching themes. Once you have your story set and you feel satisfied with the shape of it, you can refine your language, polish your sentences, and add small details for verisimilitude in subsequent drafts.

I don't recommend fine-tuning any of your sentences before you write your second draft. In fact, you might even want to wait until the third draft, depending on the complexity of your narrative.

When it's time to fine-tune effectively, though, you have to learn how to look at your story as though you weren't the one who wrote it. The challenge is to separate the story you have in your mind from what you've actually written on the page. There's the scene that exists before you write it (pre-language) and then there's the scene you've attempted to write. Your goal with this practice is to learn to read between these two scenes.

PRACTICE

Here's a quick way to see your sentences with a fresh set of eyes: read your story out loud backwards. I don't remember where I found this exercise, but it is often credited to author and writing instructor Verlyn Klinkenborg.

It's particularly useful for later-stage revision: use it when polishing sentences in a third or fourth draft.

Start with the last sentence of your story and then move through the pages one by one until you get to your first sentence. Go slow, one sentence at a time. If any sentences sound wrong or confusing, mark them with a pen so you remember where they are. You can tinker with them later.

Why does this work so well? Because if you were in a trance when you wrote your scenes, reading them the way you wrote them will only put you back into trance. Reading your sentences backwards breaks your own spell, giving you the clear eyes you need to re-envision your story.

You want every single sentence in your story to glitter with an intelligence of its own. To do this, you need to assess each sentence out of its original context. You're not going to consider the overall plot or narrative structure right now. You've already done this. Get to know each sentence intimately as an individual collection of words, sounds, images, and beats. This is how you can recognize which of your sentences need to be sharpened, without immediately worrying about how to do so.

*

PUBLISHING IN FLIGHT

Books move in murmurations, in beautiful, chaotic formations, like flocks of birds.

In a murmuration, every single bird pays attention to the six or seven birds that are closest to it, and they all adjust their speed and distance accordingly to keep from colliding. This creates mesmerizing patterns in the air—as random and elegant as the swirls of steam that rise from a hot cup of tea. One of the reasons scientists think birds do this is to confuse predators: a cloud of swirling birds makes it difficult to focus on a single target.

Sometimes science forgets that nature loves to have fun, too. If you're a creature with wings, your life depends on you dancing in the air. Your survival and your joy are entwined. What amazes me about this phenomenon is that the flight pattern is flexible, always changing, irrational, and naturally beautiful. The birds take turns leading each other.

When you think about publication, imagine your work (a book, a story, a poem) as one starling in a giant swirl of birds. The beauty of writing is that it isn't bound by space and time. And the beauty of a murmuration is that there's no plan, there's no logic: it's an organic pattern of momentum created moment by moment.

Which seven books are flying next to what you're writing right now?

Go find them. Look for published books that are similar to or in conversation with your own work. Go to your bookshelf, go to the library, peruse your local bookstore, and use their shelves to situate your work amidst seven other titles. Read them and pay attention to their movements. Syncopate and adjust your writing so you're in sync, while staying true to your own style. It's okay not to know exactly where you're all going. Enjoy the sensation of existing within a powerful flock.

*

WAITING

You puzzle over your book for some time. Your writing group loves it and gives you feedback on how to make it better. So you write another draft. You work with one or two of the revision techniques from this book. You write a third draft, and this time you feel it all come together for real. You revise it and polish each sentence until you know this is the very best book you could write.

You did it—you made it across the finish line. Success!

Motivated and energized by the momentum, you send your pitch letter to an agent you've carefully selected. You've done your research and you know that she's currently accepting manuscripts. Your book would be a perfect fit for her tastes.

This feels great. You're taking inspired action toward your dream. You notice different things: dogs wearing bow ties, glittering city lights, the vibrant green leaf of romaine lettuce. You're getting more exercise and you're listening to music with the volume turned up. You're even sleeping better. You're living the life of a writer who has written a book!

The weeks pass.

You wait for a response from the agent.

And you wait.

And you wait.

Emotions are energy in motion. When you're surfing the wave of success and feeling joyful anticipation, the vibes are positive, pulsing with the feeling of possibility. Excitement is energy that has a lot of movement.

The energy of satisfaction and contentment is a bit more chill. The beat is slower. It's a nice pace, kind of like a rumba.

When we're waiting, this beat can slow to a standstill. The combined emotions of waiting and wanting create the slowest vibration we can feel. There's no movement to the energy at all. Ask any writer—waiting feels worse than rejection. The absence of rhythm makes it feel as if you're living in a slow-motion replay. Energy is invisible, so your life looks normal to an outside observer, but everything feels heavier and slower than usual.

Waiting is part of the writing game. So how do you snap out of the sluggishness? Change the beat of your own energy.

One way to do this is by acting as if you already have what you want. If you can imagine how you'll feel after you get a positive response from an agent, and you know how to embody that energy of happiness and excitement in the present moment, do it. By embodying a faster-moving emotional state, you can lift yourself out of waiting's stalled feelings. This concept may be the origin of the phrase "Fake it till you make it."

However, shifting from zero energy (waiting) right up to high energy (excitement) in a flash is a lot to ask of your brain chemistry. Curiosity, interest, and wonder all land somewhere in between those two poles. Aim for these more accessible intermediate states to be more effective in changing your energy.

I don't believe in faking anything—to me, that's just lying to yourself, and it doesn't make me feel any better. But tapping into genuine curiosity can create movement in your energy, and doing so can bring the spirit of inquiry into the rest of your life. This just might shift your attention away from waiting and bring your energy and attention back into the world around you.

A simple, open-ended question like "Hmmm... I wonder how many houses on this street have painted their front doors a bright colour?" can change your energy. Moving your body also creates energy. If you get out of bed and go for a walk to look for coloured doors, you're already doing the work to shift out of a waiting state.

Give yourself things to do and think about while your manuscript is out on submission. Go for exploratory walks in neighbourhoods that are new to you. Volunteer at a local club, council, or organization. Learn a new language or musical instrument. Try growing herbs from seed, try new recipes, try new restaurants. Take on a new art or craft project, like visible mending, ceramics, or stained glass.

Line up a few fun things for yourself before you send your book out. You know those dream babysitters who come over with a tote bag loaded with fun stuff for a kid to play with? Do that for yourself.

The intention is to spark your mind back into curiosity after it's come to a standstill. What can you learn? What can you make? What can you count, collect, or arrange? Your creativity is always eager to take you on an adventure—it's curious about what's next.

Being a writer doesn't mean that you have to write and publish every book you finish writing right away. Write with creative curiosity when you're writing and live with creative curiosity when you're waiting. Welcome this in-between time for what it is: a chance to explore new things without limits.

*

THE OPPOSITE OF ACCEPTANCE

After waiting for some time, you've put your query and submission out of your mind. You've created a new equilibrium in your life, and your creative curiosity is back.

That's when the editor or agent finally sends their response: It's a brief and polite pass on your manuscript. A rejection letter.

This happens a lot. It happens most of the time, in fact. And it happens to all writers. Stephen King's first book, *Carrie*, was rejected thirty times before it was published. Alice Walker received numerous rejections for *The Color Purple* before it found a publisher and won the Pulitzer. One of my favourite books, *The House on Mango Street* by Sandra Cisneros, was rejected multiple times before being published—and as I write this, more than forty years later, writing teachers are still actively pressing it into the hands of their students. And Bonnie Garmus received a whopping ninety-eight rejections before her novel, *Lessons in Chemistry*, was eventually published and went on to become a bestseller.

If you're brave enough to submit your work, you'll receive rejections. And even if you're prepared to receive rejection letters, it still hurts to get one. It might even feel personal.

Ouch. Now what?

If the editor was generous enough to provide you with comments on your work, give yourself time to recognize and appreciate your feelings and reactions before you try to interpret or take action on any of their feedback. If you skip this important step, your emotional state might make it difficult to understand their notes clearly and constructively.

Spend about ten to fifteen minutes feeling whatever arises. Awareness of your own emotions will help you move through them and keep them from lingering. Then, interrupt your thoughts before they settle into a pattern. Do something that comforts your body, look at something that gives you pleasure, or talk to someone you love and let the sensation of belonging replenish you. Hang out with comfort until you feel full. When you feel safe, loved, and settled again, you can return to your work.

You submitted your writing because you wanted it to be accepted. When it wasn't, it seemed as though you got the opposite of what you wished for.

But the opposite of acceptance isn't rejection. It's resistance.

Resistance is an energy block. A fold in a garden hose can stop the flow of water, yes, but water is no less powerful because of the blocked hose.

The flow of your creative energy can be resisted and restricted, but you only have to look at the Grand Canyon to understand that the flow always wins.

After receiving a rejection letter, it can be hard to work through the resistance that might arise. If this happens to you, don't despair. This practice will help you work out the kinks in your energy's flow.

PRACTICE

Here are three simple ways to release the blocked energy and renew your flow of curiosity.

1. Write in your freewriting notebook without a specific project in mind. Write ten unconnected sentences, one after the other, and make sure that each new sentence has no relationship to the previous one. When you're finished, read them out loud and see if/how you can connect them.

2. Go to your local library or bookstore and open five books at random. Take note of the first line you read in each book—jot it down in your bullet journal or record it on your smartphone. Then read all five lines aloud, one after the other. Notice if/how they're connected.

3. Take a walk outside and look for the colour blue. Notice how your focus shifts and your perspective narrows. Once you find five blue things, switch it up and look for the colour red. Notice how it feels to switch your attention to a new colour. Once you find five red things, change your focus and look for both blue and red things at the same

time. Notice how your perspective changed in the third way of seeing, and what happens to your state of mind as you scan the landscape.

The simple power of these three practices allows you to access your superpowers of connection, separation, and meaning-making. They bring you back into a whole-minded state. Once you've returned to this state of mind, try writing something new. Let the energy rush!

*

REST·

After you leave your comfort zone, accept your fears, write a book, break it open and revise it, share it with an editor, make more revisions, and submit it for publication, it's time to take a good rest.

Give yourself some time to do nothing for a while.

But how much rest is enough?

...

Rest until you feel bored.

Rest through sadness.

Rest through doubt.

Rest through fear.

Rest even as you have a zillion new ideas.

Rest through your disappointment.

Rest through your irritation.

Rest until you feel acceptance.

. . .

When you feel your curiosity perk up again, follow it to see where it leads you.

Huh. What would happen if...

Hmm... I wonder...

Could it be possible that...

...

Let the first new ideas that come to you float around without taking action on them. Until you're fully rested, you won't know if they're valuable ideas for you to pursue.

They might be intentions left over from a previous version of yourself—the person you were before you completed your book.

...

Prioritize rest so you'll have the energy to recognize your next project, honour it with your full attention, and bring it to completion.

...

Write your ideas down in your bullet journal if you feel moved to do so.

Wait until a new idea taps you on the shoulder three times before you start working on it.

*

WRITE WHAT YOU
WANT TO READ

Writers create experiences, influence thoughts, and crystallize beliefs. We invent words for as-yet-unformed concepts, thereby making them real. We pay attention to patterns and imagine how things might play out in the future. We observe what people do when they think no one is watching. We see the details other people miss and bear witness with clear eyes so we can reveal the truth.

Writing is powerful.

When you practise your craft, you make change. Your words can make readers see what wasn't there before.

Write a story that shares something nobody else is talking about. Write a story that shows a new way to heal something that's broken. Write a story that imagines a new way for people to relate to each other, a new way to belong.

Write a story that you want to read.

You want your story to gain purchase in a world of distracted people. You want it to be more exciting than a newsfeed, more delicious than an app, full of more wonder than AI. So keep up your writing practice—the tools and techniques of your craft, when powered with creative curiosity, will give you the edge you need to captivate readers.

Once you understand the craft, I encourage you to break the rules. On purpose: You get to do whatever you want. If you don't like a certain condition or convention, change it. Maybe you'll even create a new genre.

Keep asking yourself how you want to feel about your reading and your writing. What messages have you been taking in and sending out without even realizing it? What stories, experiences, or perspectives do you wish more people would understand? What energy do you want to see more of in the world?

Write us a new story—a story that only you can write.

You might not think of yourself as a visionary, thought leader, or social change maker, but here's the thing: you are. Your work is powered by creative curiosity, discovery, dreaming, and making. You're a writer.

*

RECOMMENDED
FURTHER READING

Lynda Barry, *What It Is*

Martha Beck, *Finding Your Own North Star: Claiming the Life You Were Meant to Live*

Francesca Lia Block, *The Thorn Necklace: Healing Through Writing and the Creative Process*

Robert Olen Butler, *From Where You Dream: The Process of Writing Fiction*

Mihaly Csikszentmihalyi, *Flow: The Psychology of Optimal Experience*

Natalie Goldberg, *Writing Down the Bones: Freeing the Writer Within*

Laraine Herring, *Writing with the Breath: Embodied Writing Practice*

Scott Bary Kaufman and Carolyn Gregoire, *Wired to Create: Unraveling the Mysteries of the Creative Mind*

Stephen Nachmanovitch, *The Art of Is: Improvising as a Way of Life*

Alan Watt, *The 90-Day Novel: Unlock the Story Within*

＊

A NOTE ON
PRACTICE EXERCISES

I thoroughly enjoy working with exercises. While I've created some myself, over the years I've also gathered numerous writing practice and mindset-expanding exercises for my classes and personal development. I've collected so many that I often forget their origins.

If you recognize any exercises in this book that haven't been credited to their source—whether from a book or a teacher you've encountered—please get in touch via my website at sarahselecky.com. Your help in identifying their origins will allow me to credit them properly in future editions.

*

A NOTE ON
STUDENT EXAMPLES

Throughout this book, I occasionally draw upon experiences and insights gained from working with my students and teachers to illustrate concepts or demonstrate learning processes. To protect their privacy, I've used pseudonyms. While the essence of each example remains true to the original experience, the specific circumstances have been changed. This approach allows me to share valuable lessons and observations while respecting the confidentiality of those whose writing journeys intersected with mine.

These anonymous examples are presented with deep appreciation for all of my students, who have taught me so much about the specific challenges writers face, the power and delight that comes from a breakthrough, and the magic of collective learning.

*

THANK YOU

This book is a palimpsest, a tribute to creative energy and connection, and the culmination of over twenty years of teaching creative writing to my students. Countless individuals came together to be part of this creation over the years, and I'd like to give special thanks to some of them here.

For your wisdom, mentorship, and guidance: Natalie Goldberg, Lynda Barry, Zsuzsi Gartner, Ruth Ozeki, Al Watt, Margaret Atwood, Henry Lien, Karen Joy Fowler, Peter Levitt, Francesca Lia Block, Gillian Ferrabee, Danielle Cohen, Karen Collacutt, and Karen Kessler.

For your clarity, development, and vision: Team Assembly! Leigh Nash, Andrew Faulkner, Debby de Groot, Greg Tabor, and Stuart Ross.

For your significant contributions, support, and care: Laraib Khan, Laura Gendall, Rebecca Arango, Nailah King, Sonal Champsee, Rena Willis, Sarah Henstra, Heidi Reimer, Catherine Wright, Nora-Lyn and Terry Veevers, Kelly Cade, Annie Bray, Kate Collins, Gabriella Albino and Evan Mackenzie,

Krista Aoki and Alexis Galamay, Tammy Evans, Woz Flint, Sarah Jenkinson, Kiva Slade, Camille Ehiorobo, Christi-an Slomka, Trish Osuch, Angie Wheeler, Hannah Williams, Sam Haywood, and Pieter Swinkels.

To all of the teachers and students at the Sarah Selecky Writing School, the community of writers in Centered, my mentees, and my newsletter readers: your support, enthusiasm, and commitment to your creativity are a constant source of inspiration and growth. Thank you for embarking on this journey with me.

To the countless authors whose books have inspired me and the writing teachers whose workshops have sparked my creative curiosity: your transmission is present and alive here in these pages.

In memory of Darrel J. McLeod, whose teaching and spirit profoundly shaped our school and community. Your words continue to resonate, offering healing and release. It was an honour to fly in a murmuration with you.

To Ryan Henderson, my awe and love. You are the embodiment of creative curiosity. I learn from you every day.

*

ABOUT THE AUTHOR

Sarah Selecky began teaching creative writing because she couldn't find a workshop that taught what she truly wanted: how to achieve mastery without compromising her spirit. She is the author of the critically acclaimed novel *Radiant Shimmering Light* and the Giller Prize–shortlisted collection *This Cake Is for the Party*. As the founder of the internationally renowned Sarah Selecky Writing School, she has taught thousands of writers from around the world how to write with their intellect and intuition.

In addition to her courses, Sarah offers her beloved Story Is a State of Mind coaching and immersive retreats, providing personalized support for writers seeking to deepen their craft and creative practices.

Sarah holds an MFA from the University of British Columbia and has studied at the Banff Centre for the Arts, Hedgebrook, and the Humber School for Writers. Her first writing workshop took place in her living room in 2001, and she officially opened her school ten years later. Find her at sarahselecky.com.

PHOTO CREDIT: TARA MCMULLEN

*

ABOUT THE SARAH SELECKY WRITING SCHOOL

Since 2011, the Sarah Selecky Writing School has offered online creative writing programs renowned for their deep impact and loved by writers around the world. In 2021, we introduced Centered, a membership designed for writers who value independent work while also embracing the power of community and interdependence.

Our method blends literary craft with intuitive practice. A calm mind is a creative mind: We emphasize a writing routine that fosters presence and curiosity. We believe that writing is at its best when it brings genuine pleasure, and we encourage writers to write what they want to read.

As a compassionate alternative to traditional MFA programs, our school welcomes writers of all genres who seek to write well. We not only train writers in craft but also teach them how to regulate their nervous systems and manage anxiety, resistance, and strong emotions.

Our students grow into better writers, cultivating independent, deep, and even magical writing careers. Discover more at sarahseleckywritingschool.com.

Printed by Imprimerie Gauvin
Gatineau, Québec